Faithful Resistance

Faithful Resistance

The Seat of Moses and the
Story of Conscience in History

MIKE HENDERSON

RESOURCE *Publications* · Eugene, Oregon

FAITHFUL RESISTANCE
The Seat of Moses and the Story of Conscience in History

Copyright © 2026 Mike Henderson. All rights reserved. Except for brief quotations in critical publications or reviews, no part of this book may be reproduced in any manner without prior written permission from the publisher. Write: Permissions, Wipf and Stock Publishers, 199 W. 8th Ave., Suite 3, Eugene, OR 97401.

Resource Publications
An Imprint of Wipf and Stock Publishers
199 W. 8th Ave., Suite 3
Eugene, OR 97401

www.wipfandstock.com

PAPERBACK ISBN: 979-8-3852-7072-9
HARDCOVER ISBN: 979-8-3852-7073-6
EBOOK ISBN: 979-8-3852-7074-3

Scripture quotations marked (NIV) are taken from *The Holy Bible, New International Version*®, *NIV*®. Copyright © 1973, 1978, 1984, 2011 by Biblica, Inc.™ Used by permission. All rights reserved worldwide.

To Charlie Kirk—
who walked into darkness to speak light,
and to all who refused to bow when conscience was on trial:
the prophets, the apostles, the reformers,
and the faithful whose names history may never record.
And to Shirley—
whose quiet strength and steadfast faith
have been my living example of faithful resistance.

"For the law was given through Moses; grace and truth came through Jesus Christ."

(John 1:17)

Contents

Preface ix

Acknowledgments xiii

MOVEMENT I — *The Foundation of the Seat*

1 — The Law That Was Perfect from God 3

2 — The Journey of the Seat 6

3 — From Ceremony to Relationship 10

4 — The Tension of the Seat: Christ as Fulfillment 13

MOVEMENT II — *The Fulfillment and the Church*

5 — The Sword and the Cross 19

6 — The Body and the Bride 24

7 — Measured Resistance: The Threefold Path of Conscience 27

8 — The Doctrine of Conscience 31

9 — The Witness of John: Light, Truth, and Resistance 36

10 — The Law of Sin and God's Law 43

MOVEMENT III — *The Seat Through History*

11 — The Law of Redemptive Resistance: Conscience as the Seed of Renewal 59

12 — The Failure of Church and State: When Conscience Became a Captive 63

CONTENTS

13 — Conscience Under Creed: Lessons from Geneva 68

14 — Christ Among the Lampstands 72

MOVEMENT IV — *The Restoration of Conscience*

15 — The Seat Within 81

16 — The Faith of Faithful Resistance 87

17 — Truth and Coercion 92

Epilogue: The Freedom of the Faithful 99

Postlude: The Story of Conscience 101

Appendix I: Separation of Church and State 105

Appendix II: The Prophetic Voice 111

Appendix III: The Watchman's Seat 117

Appendix IV: Consciousness and Divine Order: The Soul and Spirit in God's Created Field 121

Appendix V: The Machine Without Conscience 128

Appendix VI: Predestination, Eternity, and the Category Error That Distorts the Father 134

Appendix VII: The Lineage of Holy Conscience: An Index of Witnesses 140

Index 149

Preface

Faithful Resistance began with a single question: What does it mean to obey God when those in power misuse his name?

That question has echoed through every age of the church—from prophets who warned kings to reformers who stood before councils. It is the question of conscience, the inner seat of moral law where the soul meets the voice of God. From Sinai to this present hour, that voice has called the faithful not to rebellion but to righteousness, not to pride but to endurance. The greatest revolutions in history were not started by armies but by hearts unwilling to call evil good.

From the order first spoken in creation to the law inscribed on stone, from the long silence between prophets to the Word made flesh, and from the cross to the renewal of all things, the story of conscience has never ceased. The same voice that formed the world still calls it to righteousness. In every age—revealed, tested, fulfilled, and awaiting restoration—the law of God continues its witness through the hearts of those who hear and obey.

> Matt 23:2—"The teachers of the law and the Pharisees sit in Moses' seat."

When Christ spoke of the *seat of Moses*, he referred not to a single chair of authority but to an enduring pattern—the unfolding of divine order through time. Fourteen hundred years had passed since Moses first sat in judgment, and the pattern still held. The seat marks the meeting point of law, mercy, and accountability. From the mountain where the law was given, to the temple where it was misused, and onward into the conscience of every believer, it stands as witness that all earthly power answers to heaven.

In the synagogues of Jesus' day, this pattern took physical form in what was called "the seat of Moses," the recognized place from which the Scriptures were read and explained. It was not a literal throne of Moses, but a teaching chair symbolizing the authority God gave him to speak his law to the people. When Jesus referred to this seat (Matt 23:2-3), he affirmed the legitimacy of that teaching authority even as he condemned the hypocrisy of those who misused it. Understanding the seat of Moses shows that God cares not only that truth is proclaimed, but that its teachers are themselves submitted to the Spirit who gave the law.

WHY THE STORY UNFOLDS IN FOUR MOVEMENTS

This book follows the long arc of God's work in history through four movements—each one a deeper turn into the same truth. They are not new doctrines, nor alternate interpretations, but successive layers of sight. Each movement draws the reader further into the moral order of God: from law revealed, to law fulfilled, to conscience awakened, to faithful resistance lived. The movements build, not by changing direction, but by deepening vision—showing how God governs the soul, the church, and the city through the same enduring truth.

MOVEMENT I—THE FOUNDATION OF THE SEAT (CHAPTERS 1-4)

The story begins where all conscience begins—with revelation. At Sinai, the law descended not as tyranny but as light. It revealed the moral architecture of creation and entrusted divine authority to human stewardship. Even then, the law pointed beyond itself to mercy—to the day when the Giver of the law would bear its judgment himself. Here the seat is established: the meeting place of holiness and humanity, where obedience becomes the first act of freedom.

MOVEMENT II—THE FULFILLMENT AND THE CHURCH (CHAPTERS 5-10)

The second movement turns from the mountain to the cross. At Calvary, law and love meet in perfect union. The church was born from that union—not as an instrument of control but as the body through which the Spirit governs conscience from within. Here believers learn the triad of faithful response: to flee evil, to endure under unjust power, and, when called, to resist in truth. In this movement, law and love unite, and conscience learns to govern both soul and society under grace.

MOVEMENT III—THE SEAT THROUGH HISTORY (CHAPTERS 11-14)

From the early church to modern republics, the seat of Moses reappears in new forms—always contested, always preserved. The history of nations is the history of that contest: power attempting to silence truth, church and state forgetting their limits, and reformers rising to recall both to righteousness. Whenever power forgets humility, conscience rises to restore it; whenever law is misused, grace rekindles its light.

MOVEMENT IV—THE RESTORATION OF CONSCIENCE (CHAPTERS 15-17)

The final movement returns the seat to its rightful throne—the human heart purified by grace. Here conscience stands renewed, free from coercion yet bound to truth. The story culminates not in triumphalism but in transformation: the church refined, the soul reawakened, and the Spirit breathing liberty where fear once ruled.

The same Voice that shook Sinai now gathers the field. Truth and freedom stand reconciled, and the harvest of redemption begins.

THE READER'S INVITATION

The reader is invited to hear not just history but harmony. These four movements are not distant eras but living rhythms within every soul that seeks to walk uprightly before God. They reveal how divine authority moves through time—descending as law, suffering as grace, contending through conscience, and rising again as restored truth.

Faithful Resistance is not a call to political defiance but to spiritual fidelity. The true conflict is not between church and state but between pride and obedience, coercion and conscience, darkness and light. The weapons of this warfare are not forged by human hands—they are truth, love, and the law fulfilled in Christ: the divine order that governs creation even when creation resists it.

Each chapter serves as both mirror and measure. Within its pages the reader will see the same pattern repeating through the ages: law revealed, law corrupted, conscience awakened, redemption restored. Beneath that pattern runs the unbroken melody of divine government—the steady hand of God reclaiming his throne within the human heart.

Faithful Resistance is the story of that restoration: the rediscovery of the law written not on stone but upon the soul, the triumph of grace where judgment once ruled. To every reader approaching these pages in prayer, may your conscience be quickened, your courage renewed, and your hope secured. For the day will come when the seat of Moses yields to the throne of the Lamb, and the kingdoms of this world become the kingdom of our Lord and of his Christ.

Guard your heart—for there sits the seat of God.

Acknowledgments

No work of conscience is ever written alone. Though the words upon these pages bear my name, the faith and friendship of many have guided their shaping.

To Shirley—whose steadfast heart and quiet courage have been both mirror and measure of all I hoped this book would express—your faith has been my teacher, your patience my guardrail, your love my rest.

To my family and friends who have carried me through seasons of silence and renewal—you have been living examples of faithful resistance: gentle in conviction, strong in grace.

To the pastors, teachers, and fellow watchmen who keep the lamp burning in darkened times—thank you for holding the line where truth and mercy meet. The seat of Moses still stands because hearts like yours still kneel before the Lord who spoke from it.

To those who came before—reformers, prophets, scholars, and saints—this book is an echo of your obedience. You taught us that truth cannot be silenced, even when its stewards are.

Above all, I give thanks to the Holy Spirit, whose quiet revelation has been the true source of every insight found here. Whatever light these pages hold did not begin in me but was given—sometimes in stillness, sometimes in struggle—by the One who teaches truth to every willing heart.

And finally, to the reader:

If these pages kindle your conscience toward courage or turn your gaze from fear to faith, then this work has fulfilled its purpose. May the light that guided me now guide you, until we all stand before the throne of him whose kingdom needs no resistance—because it knows no corruption.

> Rom 16:27—"To the only wise God be glory forever through Jesus Christ. Amen."

Movement I—
The Foundation of the Seat

"The mountain still burns, and the voice still speaks."
—*Faithful Resistance*, ch. 1

CHAPTER 1

The Law That Was Perfect from God

Exod 19:18—"The mountain trembled violently, and the sound of the trumpet grew louder and louder. Then Moses spoke and the voice of God answered him."

The law began not in the mind of man but in the mouth of God. It was not negotiated or reasoned into existence; it was revealed. When the Lord descended upon Sinai in fire, the mountain became the first pulpit of the world—stone turned to covenant, silence to command. What chaos had undone since Eden, divine speech began to restore. For the order once written into creation was now spoken again upon the mountain—the same moral breath that shaped the garden now carved itself in stone. Even as the law thundered, grace was already present, for the revelation of order was itself an act of mercy. It taught fallen hearts how to live within the design of their Maker. The commandments were not chains but structure—the moral form of love expressed through justice. To obey was not to surrender to tyranny but to walk within truth.

  Faith is the soul's first obedience—the inward assent to divine order before a single command is kept. It is the bridge between revelation and response, the moment when the heart believes that the voice from the mountain speaks to it as surely as to creation. The revelation at Sinai still speaks. It declares that morality is not a human invention but a recognition of divine order. It reminds us that justice without holiness collapses into self-righteousness, and conscience without humility crowns itself king. The law exposes sin not to destroy life but to preserve it, for darkness is only known as darkness when light defines it.

When Scripture speaks of "the law," it does not speak of a single rule book but of a unified revelation expressed in distinct ways. The moral law revealed God's unchanging character—commands that showed what goodness looks like in every age. The civil law ordered Israel's life as a nation—its courts, penalties, and public justice. The ceremonial law prepared the heart for Christ—through sacrifices, priests, and a temple that pointed beyond itself. Jesus did not abolish these layers; he fulfilled the ceremonial shadows and upheld the moral truth they carried. Many new believers imagine the law as one indistinguishable whole, but God revealed it in different forms so that every part of life—worship, justice, and morality—would be shaped by his holiness.

From the beginning, God's intent was covenantal: "I will be your God, and you will be my people." The law was relationship before it was regulation. Its commands trained the soul toward communion—obedience as worship, righteousness as love. The sacrifices and feasts were lessons in holiness, shadows of a redemption not yet seen, preparing the heart to receive mercy. But holiness mishandled becomes danger. Israel's priests were called to guard the altar; over time they mistook stewardship for ownership. By the days of Christ, the Sanhedrin guarded the letter of the law while losing its light. They sat in Moses' seat but forgot the God who once sat upon the mountain. The lawgiver stood before them, and they judged the Judge.

Thus the law that was perfect from God was placed in the hands of imperfect men so that failure would reveal the need for grace. Every commandment pointed beyond itself; every sacrifice spoke of the One to come. When Christ ascended the Mount of Beatitudes and opened his mouth, the mountain spoke again—not in thunder but in mercy. The same voice that once carved words into stone now wrote them upon the heart. The mountain still burns, not with wrath but with witness, and the law that was perfect from God continues to write itself upon every conscience that bows before him. In that humility, the fire of Sinai becomes the light of the soul—the beginning of faithful resistance and the first lesson of a redeemed heart.

REFLECTION

Sinai still stands in spirit, its summit veiled but its voice unbroken. Every conscience awakened by God's command stands again on that mountain, caught between fear and wonder. The fire that once burned on stone now burns within the heart. The God who once wrote with his finger now writes by his Spirit. Law was never the enemy of love but its form—love structured and revealed through order. To meditate on the commandments is to remember that holiness is not cruelty but clarity, heaven's order spoken into earth's confusion. The law calls us not to perfection through effort but to purity through dependence. To hear that call is to return to the Source—to bow before the voice that once spoke light into being and now speaks truth into the soul.

CALL TO FAITHFUL RESISTANCE—THE LAW THAT STILL SPEAKS

Faithful resistance begins where the heart chooses truth over ease—where conscience bows to God rather than culture. Let the church stand again as a living Sinai—holy not from fear but from love rightly ordered. The Word that once shook the mountain still governs the soul.

> Jas 1:22—"Do not merely listen to the word, and so deceive yourselves. Do what it says."

Let obedience prove faith. Reject belief without action. Test conviction by what it produces. Live the Word you profess. Let conscience be verified in deed, not in speech alone.

CHAPTER 2

The Journey of the Seat

> Deut 16:18—"Appoint judges and officials for each of your tribes in every town the Lord your God is giving you, and they shall judge the people fairly."

The seat of Moses did not remain at Sinai. It journeyed with the people—first carried through the wilderness by memory, then established in the promised land by mandate. It was more than a seat; it was the visible conscience of a nation, a continual reminder that judgment belongs to God and that every ruler is only a steward of his moral throne. When Israel was commanded to appoint judges and officials, the instruction was not political innovation but spiritual trust. Authority was to reflect the righteousness of heaven. Each judge ruled by delegation; every verdict was to echo the divine character. The lawgiver, the Judge, and the King were never to be divided in purpose, for they are one in the nature of God himself (Isa 33:22).

Every ruling was a sacred echo. Each decision carried eternal consequence. The judge was not free to rule by emotion, for emotion shifts with the crowd; he was bound to the unchanging Word. The fear of the Lord became the beginning of justice. Where conscience ruled the gavel, righteousness prospered; but where ambition replaced awe, the seat itself began to shake. As generations passed, that unity fractured. The elders of Israel demanded a king "like the nations" (1 Sam 8:5). They sought safety in power rather than in Presence. The seat that once faced heaven turned toward the thrones of men.

When justice turned its gaze earthward, the poor disappeared from view. Bribes silenced widows, and influence drowned out prayer. The law that had protected the weak became a shield for the strong. Authority shifted from stewardship to self-preservation. The throne still bore Scripture, but its heart grew cold to the God who wrote it. The Sanhedrin that emerged centuries later carried both covenant and corruption. Charged to uphold the law, it often used that law to preserve privilege, suppress truth, and defend its own authority.

Through the prophets, God called his people back to moral center. Elijah on Carmel, Isaiah in the temple, and Jeremiah at the gate stood before kings as living reminders that no human decree can cancel divine justice. Each prophet resisted in his own way—Elijah through confrontation, Isaiah through consecration, Jeremiah through lamentation—but all obeyed the same law of conscience: truth before comfort, fidelity before favor. Every prophet became a living seat of Moses, confronting power with conscience and warning that covenant cannot survive without compassion.

Even prophetic courage met resistance. When priesthood hardened into privilege, the seat became a stage. Judgment could be bought, and mercy was rationed. The covenant remained in parchment but not in practice. What once symbolized moral order began to mirror political order. The law written on stone was buried beneath the laws written by men. Yet the remnant remembered. Their faith no longer depended on a court or a country. In exile they carried the law not in scrolls but in hearts, discovering that conscience cannot be conquered by distance. In Babylon they learned new tongues but not new loyalties. In Persia they gained favor but did not forget covenant. Daniel's prayer in Babylon and Esther's plea before a foreign throne proved that faithful resistance is possible even when the seat is held by the unworthy.

Centuries passed, and the echo of Sinai faded beneath layers of ritual and rule. Yet the covenant endured, waiting for fulfillment. By the time Christ entered the temple, the seat of Moses had become both sacred and hollow. Those who claimed it recited truth but failed to recognize Truth standing before them. Yet Jesus did not destroy the seat—he affirmed its origin and exposed its hypocrisy. "The teachers of the law and the Pharisees sit in Moses' seat," he said. "So you must be careful to do everything they tell you. But do not do what they do, for they do not practice what they preach" (Matt 23:2-3). His rebuke was not of authority itself but of those who corrupted it.

The journey of the seat ends in paradox: authority remains holy even when its holders are not. God's order endures through flawed vessels, preserving the pattern until the perfect Judge appears. The seat once carved in stone would soon be revealed in flesh—the moral law embodied, not in tablets or thrones, but in the life of the Son. In him, divine authority and human conscience met face to face. The path from Sinai to Calvary is the pilgrimage of authority itself—from commandment to compassion, from decree to deliverance. The seat of Moses, tested by kings and prophets, finds its final dwelling not in the temple but in the heart of Christ. Through him, the journey begins anew—its destination no longer a nation's court but the conscience of the redeemed.

The seat demands more than obedience; it requires alignment. Every generation must decide whether authority will serve heaven or self. That line is not drawn in law books but in the soul.

CALL TO FAITHFUL RESISTANCE—THE BURDEN OF STEWARDS

Every bearer of authority faces the same danger that shadowed Israel's elders—the temptation to protect position instead of purity. Faithful resistance begins not with condemning rulers but with ruling oneself. To steward power humbly is the first rebellion against pride. May we, like Moses, choose intercession over ambition and remember that the seat of Moses was never a throne of self but a trust from God.

> Deuteronomy 16:20—"Follow justice and justice alone, so that you may live and possess the land the Lord your God is giving you."

Uphold justice even when power tempts compromise. Do not imitate authority that forgets righteousness. Judge by truth, not by advantage. Keep integrity before influence. Let justice—not fear—govern the conscience.

CHAPTER 3

From Ceremony to Relationship

Matt 9:13—"Go and learn what this means:
'I desire mercy, not sacrifice.'"

"Authority is holy only when it kneels."
—*Faithful Resistance*, ch. 3

The law that thundered at Sinai was never meant to end in ritual. The sacrifices, washings, feasts, and fasts were shadows of a reality still unseen—a discipline that trained the heart to recognize its need for redemption. Each ceremony was a reminder of Eden, a rehearsal for restoration, a sign that fellowship with God was not lost but awaiting renewal. Yet within every repetition stirred a deeper ache. The people performed the form but longed for the Presence. Even in the fragrance of incense they felt distance; even in obedience they felt absence. The ceremony preserved holiness, but it could not restore intimacy. What ritual maintained, relationship still awaited. The hunger was not for less law but for living law—a covenant written not on parchment but in presence.

The priesthood carried that longing in its hands. Every lamb laid upon the altar spoke the same truth: this is not enough. The blood of bulls and goats could symbolize forgiveness but could not impart it. The temple preserved memory, not life. It guarded access to God but could not grant it. The world's center of worship remained active, but the heart of man stayed divided. When Christ came, the shadow met the substance. The veil that divided the holy from the common revealed not God's distance but man's unreadiness. When Jesus said, "Destroy this temple, and I will raise it again in three days," he revealed that the true temple was his own body—the meeting place of heaven and earth, where mercy and justice embraced.

The priests asked for ritual; he offered relationship. They sought ceremony to preserve control; he offered communion to restore life. "I desire mercy, not sacrifice" was not the rejection of worship but its correction. Mercy is worship in motion—holiness expressed through compassion, truth lived through love. The perfection of the cross was not in the precision of its form but in the purity of its purpose. Love accomplished what law only described. Where the priest washed his hands, Christ opened his. Where the sacrifice was repeated daily, he offered himself once for all. The difference was not ceremonial but moral: love fulfilled what ritual could only prefigure.

Thus, the ceremonial law bowed before the relational grace it anticipated. Incense, offerings, and purifications found their completion in the cross. There, the Lamb became both priest and sacrifice, altar and mercy seat. The shadow yielded to the light. The symbols were not destroyed; they were fulfilled. The early church understood this not as doctrine alone but as transformation. Baptism replaced the laver. Communion replaced the altar. The heart became the temple. What had been the ceremony of approach became the indwelling of presence. The law once written on scrolls was now written on hearts by the Spirit of the living God (2 Cor 3:3).

But the danger remained. The human impulse to ritualize relationship persists. Whenever form is exalted above faith or performance above purity, the ceremony returns and the relationship retreats. Even in the church, the old temptation survives—to serve at the altar of propriety rather than the altar of love. Modern believers may not burn incense, but they often mistake performance for presence—honoring the ceremony while neglecting the Lord.

True worship is not skill but surrender. Its music is measured not by sound but by motive. God is not moved by performance but by purity.

Christ's fulfillment calls his followers to simplicity and sincerity—to worship in spirit and in truth, not merely in sequence and tradition. The seat of conscience is not a platform for spectacle but a sanctuary for presence. Every sacrament that endures does so only because it points beyond itself to the One who fulfilled it. From ceremony to relationship, from shadow to substance, the path of redemption remains the same: God descending to dwell with man, and man rising to walk with God. The torn veil still speaks. The temple curtain, ripped from top to bottom, is not a relic of history but a declaration of proximity. God is near. Holiness no longer dwells in stone but in the believer whose heart has become his dwelling place.

CALL TO FAITHFUL RESISTANCE—THE INNER THRONE

When ritual becomes routine, the soul drifts from Presence. The altar without the heart is empty stone. Faithful resistance is the return from performance to presence—from law observed to love obeyed. Let the believer cleanse the inner temple so that worship again becomes witness.

> Rom 2:15—"They show that the requirements of the law are written on their hearts, their consciences also bearing witness."

Listen when conscience convicts before others do. Let moral law, not emotion, direct your choices. Guard the voice within—it is God's witness in you. Refuse the excuses that silence conviction. Act as one already seen by God.

CHAPTER 4

The Tension of the Seat: Christ as Fulfillment

Matt 5:17—"Do not think that I have come to abolish the Law or the Prophets; I have not come to abolish them but to fulfill them."

The seat of Moses, carved by covenant and carried through generations, came to its fulfillment in Christ. Here the law met the One who wrote it. The voice that thundered from Sinai now spoke in a Galilean street. The same hand that carved commandments in stone now traced mercy in dust. The divine authority that once judged from the mountain now stooped to heal the broken and cleanse the unclean.

Christ did not abolish the law; he embodied it. Every command found its center in him. Justice took the form of compassion. Purity became restoration. Truth was revealed through grace. Yet in him also appeared the enduring tension of Israel's story—the strain between confrontation and compassion, between judgment and mercy, between the sword and the shepherd's staff.

When Jesus cleansed the temple, he was not rejecting law but restoring it. The tables he overturned represented transaction without transformation—religion without repentance. His zeal consumed him because his Father's house had become a market instead of a meeting place. That act of holy disruption revealed the seat of Moses purified by love: authority exercised not for control but for cleansing.

This is the tension of faithful resistance. To confront evil under God's authority is not rebellion; it is obedience. Peter's sword, raised in fear, was rebuked—but the same Peter later preached with fire, wielding the sword of truth. John the Baptist told soldiers not to abandon their swords but to use them righteously. The difference lies not in the weapon but in the motive of the heart.

Christ demonstrated perfect authority under perfect submission. He could summon legions but chose silence. He could condemn with justice but chose to redeem through suffering. Each wound testified; each silence instructed—the justice of God written in Mercy's own blood. In his submission, authority was not diminished but exalted. On the cross, he fulfilled every office—Lawgiver, Judge, and King—by surrendering to the Father's will. There, the seat of Moses became the mercy seat of heaven. Judgment was transformed into intercession, power into peace.

In Christ, divine authority and human obedience are reconciled. The threefold law—moral, civil, and ceremonial—finds its unity restored. What humanity divided, Christ made whole. Grace does not weaken the law; it magnifies it. The commandments are not abolished but completed in love. From this fulfillment arises the standard of all faithful resistance: to stand in truth without pride, to obey conscience without rebellion, to exercise influence without domination. The Christian lives in that tension—a citizen of heaven serving within the world, a steward of moral authority bearing the humility of the cross.

The seat of Moses was never meant to exalt men but to reveal God. In Christ, that purpose is complete. The authority of heaven has been clothed in human compassion. The King reigns from the cross, and the conscience of his people becomes his throne. The lawgiver now lives within the heart. The mountain has moved to the soul. The voice that once spoke in thunder now speaks through conscience, calling every generation to walk in the same harmony—strength restrained by righteousness, truth expressed through mercy, authority redeemed by love.

THE TENSION OF THE SEAT: CHRIST AS FULFILLMENT

The fulfillment of the law is not only a mystery to contemplate but a mandate to live. What Christ completed in himself, he continues through the conscience of his people.

CALL TO FAITHFUL RESISTANCE—THE LAWGIVER WITHIN

If the lawgiver lives within you, will you still wait for others to act before you obey? The thunder of Sinai has become the whisper of conscience. When that voice speaks, hesitation is disobedience. What altar, habit, or fear must be laid down so that law and love may again be one within you? Revelation fulfilled requires incarnation—truth lived through obedience.

> Isa 5:20—"Woe to those who call evil good and good evil, who put darkness for light and light for darkness."

Name evil for what it is, even when culture applauds it. Refuse language that conceals sin. Do not trade clarity for comfort. Guard your words; they either heal or deceive. Let moral truth remain unmixed.

Conscience is where God speaks to the individual; authority is where God restrains the world. These two cannot be separated without the collapse of both. Having seen what conscience is and why Christ guards it, we now turn to the structures that surround it—the authorities that wield the sword, the institutions that govern our common life, and the limits God himself places upon them.

Movement II—The Fulfillment and the Church

"Power is tested not by how it rules, but by how it listens."
—*Faithful Resistance*, ch. 5

CHAPTER 5

The Sword and the Cross

Luke 22:36—"But now if you have a purse, take it, and also a bag; and if you don't have a sword, sell your cloak and buy one."

When Christ told his disciples to buy a sword, heaven and earth met in a single command. The Lord who healed an enemy's wound spoke of a weapon. The Teacher of Peace mentioned steel. From that night forward, the conscience of the faithful has lived within this tension.

For three years the disciples followed the Prince of Peace. They learned that meekness is not weakness and mercy is not retreat. They saw him still storms and silence demons, yet never strike in vengeance. But on the night before the cross, he prepared them for a hostile world. "If you don't have a sword, sell your cloak and buy one." The command was not rebellion but readiness—arming conscience, not campaign.

The sword is the sign of power; the cross is the sign of restraint. Between them lies the field where conscience must stand. To bear the sword without the cross is to become the oppressor one resists. To bear the cross without readiness is to abandon the innocent. Faithful resistance requires both—the courage to confront evil and the humility to suffer for righteousness.

The disciples misunderstood, as many still do. When the guards seized Jesus, Peter drew his sword and struck. The act was brave but blind. "Put your sword back in its place," Christ said, "for all who draw the sword will die by the sword." (Matt 26:52). Power without obedience destroys itself.

Yet Jesus did not despise the sword; he sanctified its purpose. "If my kingdom were of this world, my servants would fight," he told Pilate (see John 18:36). In those words, he drew the boundary between coercion and conviction. The sword may defend the innocent, but it may never advance the gospel.

The tension remains: how to live in a fallen world that demands both mercy and might. The state bears the sword to restrain evil (Rom 13:4); the church bears the cross to redeem it. When either confuses its role, tyranny follows. The disciple must therefore walk the narrow path between pacifism and presumption. The Christian weapon is conscience—formed by truth, guided by law, and surrendered to God.

From the beginning, the struggle to hold the sword rightly has defined humanity. Cain raised it in envy, Abraham drew it in rescue, David wielded it in covenant defense. Scripture never glorifies violence, but it affirms justice. The question is not whether the sword exists, but whose hand holds it and under what spirit it moves.

John the Baptist understood this. When soldiers asked him, "What should we do?" he answered, "Do not extort and be content with your pay" (Luke 3:14). He did not reject their vocation; he purified it. The sword was not to be discarded but disciplined. Authority could serve righteousness when governed by conscience.

Peter's story followed the same lesson. He began with a blade and ended with a pen. His strength was not denied, only redirected. The hand that once drew steel came to bear the keys of the kingdom. Moral force must pass through repentance before it becomes spiritual authority.

Across centuries the faithful have wrestled with this question: how to confront evil without becoming its image. Moses stood before Pharaoh with a staff, not a sword. Deborah judged Israel through moral clarity that summoned courage. Daniel resisted tyranny through truth and prayer. Their strength lay not in arms but in conviction.

At times, however, the sword was necessary. Prophets were slain, saints hunted, and tyrants demanded worship. When persecution came, the faithful sometimes fought—not to conquer, but to protect. Self-defense and the defense of the innocent are rooted in divine justice.

Even within Rome's legions, believers lived by conscience. The centurion Cornelius believed while still in uniform. In AD 286, the Theban Legion, a unit of Egyptian Christian soldiers, refused to sacrifice to Roman gods and were martyred in obedience. They served with integrity, knowing all power answers to God.

As empires rose, the struggle deepened. When Constantine merged throne and altar, the sword of the state began to wear the cross. Crusades and inquisitions followed—proof that when the cross is chained to empire, both are defiled. Yet even then, a remnant remembered that true defense is measured by mercy.

From the martyrs of Rome to the Reformers before kings, the faithful learned that the greatest weapon is integrity. Conscience, shaped by Scripture and refined by suffering, divides falsehood from truth and fear from faith. It compels obedience to God rather than coercion by men.

The cross is the measure of every sword. It stands at history's center as the judgment seat of love—where justice and mercy met without contradiction. The nails that fixed Christ's hands restrained vengeance and revealed true strength: power submitted to righteousness. In his surrender, the weapon of justice was remade as the instrument of grace.

From that moment, every sword found its meaning. The blade that once symbolized dominion became a mirror of sacrifice. Christ bore no weapon yet conquered all. He wore no crown of gold yet reigned from thorns. His victory was not in taking life but in giving it. Since that hour, every act of force must be judged by the cross—its motive, its measure, and its mercy.

Those who would take up the sword must first kneel beneath the cross. There conscience is tested—not just "Do I have the right?" but "Am I right before God?" The question of resistance is never answered by impulse, only by obedience. Power must always bow to love. It may defend, but never dominate. It may restrain, but never rejoice in blood.

The cross also measures submission. To suffer wrongfully for righteousness is not weakness but moral strength. The apostles resisted not with rebellion but with testimony. They obeyed God rather than men (Acts 5:29) and accepted the cost without complaint. Their suffering became the seed of renewal, their death the harvest of freedom.

Through the cross, the faithful learn that resistance is not rejection of authority but refusal of corruption. It is conscience standing upright when all else bows. It is Daniel before Darius, Stephen before the Sanhedrin, Luther before the emperor—men without swords who wielded truth as their defense.

Each generation must rediscover this balance: the sword in its sheath, the cross in its heart. The believer is called neither to retreat nor revolt, but to measured resistance—the defense of innocence, the endurance of injustice when conscience requires.

The state still bears the sword to restrain lawlessness; the church still bears the cross to redeem it. When joined under Christ, justice breathes. When divided, tyranny or anarchy prevails. The sword without the cross becomes a tyrant's tool; the cross without the sword becomes an escape from duty. When rightly held under conscience, the sword is mercy in motion—protecting life until love can heal it.

Faithful resistance lives in that tension—a readiness ruled by restraint. It defends what is holy without hatred and endures what is unjust without surrender. Its strength is love disciplined by law. Its courage is peace that does not yield to fear.

The world measures victory by conquest; heaven measures it by conscience. The sword may win a war, but only the cross ends enmity. Our age stands again where Peter once stood—between zeal and surrender, between the impulse to defend truth by force and the call to reveal it by faith. Only the cross teaches the difference.

From the garden where will first wavered, to the mountain where law first thundered, to the cross where mercy triumphed, the same divine order endures—the Word ruling creation not by might, but by conscience reconciled to love. In that holy paradox lies the believer's call: to carry both—the cross that redeems and the sword that defends—until the day when neither is needed, for righteousness shall dwell upon the earth.

CALL TO FAITHFUL RESISTANCE—THE PERIL OF THE HOLY SWORD

The calling to bear the sword is no small trust. God entrusts it to restrain evil, protect the innocent, and preserve order until the day when perfect justice reigns. The hand that holds it must therefore tremble before heaven even as it stands firm on earth. The sword may defend, but it must never dominate; it may strike, but never for pride. When guided by conscience, it becomes mercy in motion—protecting life until love can heal it. The church betrays her mission when she trades prayer for policy as her power, or faith for force as her method. The sword can restrain evil but cannot restore good. It can defend the innocent but cannot sanctify the guilty. Let the church remember: the cross saves what the sword cannot, and the Lamb conquers by truth, not by violence.

> Mic 6:8—"He has shown you, O mortal, what is good. And what does the Lord require of you? To act justly and to love mercy and to walk humbly with your God."

Judge with humility, not superiority. Hold mercy and justice together. Let righteousness begin in your own dealings. Defend the weak without pride. Serve God's judgment through compassion.

The sword was given to restrain evil, not to imitate it. Yet history shows that when authority forgets its limits, the sword becomes an idol in the hands of men. Before we can understand why conscience must resist the misuse of power, we must look at the moments when the sword ceased to protect the innocent and began to punish the faithful.

CHAPTER 6

The Body and the Bride

Eph 5:25–27—"Christ loved the church and gave himself up for her to make her holy, cleansing her by the washing with water through the word, and to present her to himself as a radiant church, without stain or wrinkle or any other blemish, but holy and blameless."

The law fulfilled in Christ did not vanish when he ascended. It took living form. What had once been written on tablets and scrolls now lived within redeemed hearts. The Spirit that descended at Pentecost was the same voice that thundered at Sinai—no longer above men, but within them. The church was born that day, not as an institution but as the continuation of Christ's own conscience in the world.

She is called the body of Christ because she bears his presence, and the bride of Christ because she bears his purity. Through her, the moral order revealed in the law and fulfilled in the cross is made visible. Her authority is moral, not political; persuasive, not coercive. When she is faithful, she becomes the conscience of nations. When she is corrupt, she reflects their decay.

From the beginning, her power was paradoxical. She conquered without armies, ruled without thrones, and governed through grace. Her King wore no crown of gold, yet emperors feared his name. The apostles, unarmed and uncredentialed, carried greater authority than Caesar's legions—the authority of truth. Their message was not new ideology but restored creation: Christ enthroned in the human conscience.

But this trust was tested. As the church grew, she faced the same temptations that had undone Israel—pride of ceremony and lust for control. When she forgot her dependence, she sought to rule. When she forgot her purity, she sought approval. In every generation, the struggle between the body's humility and the bride's adornment has shaped her witness.

To be the body is to suffer with Christ; to be the bride is to be sanctified by him. These are not two callings but one vocation of love. The Spirit that unites believers to Christ also unites them to one another. The church is not a gathering of individuals but a living organism—one conscience, one faith, one Spirit.

When Paul wrote that Christ "gave himself up for her," he spoke of sacrifice, not sentiment. The church is made holy not by prosperity but by purification. The washing of water through the word is a continual cleansing—a lifelong return to the truth that authority flows only from submission. The bride's beauty is moral, not ornamental. Her radiance is obedience.

In every age, God calls his people to guard this identity. The church must live in the world without becoming of it—light distinct from darkness even while dispelling it. Her strength lies not in conformity but in contrast. She confronts evil not with hostility but with holiness; not by domination but by demonstration.

The adornment of the bride is her integrity. When the church walks in purity, she exposes corruption simply by existing. When she lives in truth, she liberates conscience. When she submits to Christ, she stands above kings.

Today the old temptation returns in new forms—marketing over mission, influence over integrity. The church does not need the world's approval to change it. She was not called to imitate but to illuminate.

The body and the bride are one: the visible and invisible church, the servant and the beloved. Together they reveal Christ's continuing work in history—his authority embodied, his conscience alive, his holiness present. In her faithfulness, law and grace remain joined. In her unfaithfulness, they appear divided. The world watches to see which she will choose.

Holiness is not withdrawal but presence undefiled—the church in the world as light in darkness, clear yet compassionate.

CALL TO FAITHFUL RESISTANCE—THE DISCIPLINE OF THE SOUL

The bride of Christ is adorned not in splendor but in surrender. Her purity preserves her power. The believer who disciplines his heart guards the beauty of the church. To walk in holiness is the most radical defiance of hell. Let every soul who bears his name depart from iniquity, that grace may shine unshadowed in her midst.

> Deut 17:19–20—"It is to be with him, and he is to read it all the days of his life . . . so that he may learn to revere the Lord his God."

Let every leader be governed by God's word. Resist authority that forgets accountability. Pray for rulers, but do not worship them. Honor office while obeying truth. Fear God more than the crown.

CHAPTER 7

Measured Resistance: The Threefold Path of Conscience

Acts 5:29—"Peter and the other apostles replied: 'We must obey God rather than human beings!'"

"Conscience is not rebellion but remembrance of God's voice."
—*Faithful Resistance*, ch. 7

Conscience is not a passive faculty. It speaks, commands, and—when rightly formed—obeys. But obedience is never unthinking. It listens to two voices: the voice of authority and the voice of God. When those voices diverge, conscience must choose. That choice, made again and again through history, defines the faith of the church.

From the beginning, God's people have faced rulers who demanded what he forbade or forbade what he required. The pattern for those moments has already been given. Scripture reveals three faithful responses to unjust authority: to flee, to disobey yet submit, and to resist faithfully. Each honors God. Each requires discernment.

1. TO FLEE—THE PATH OF PRESERVATION

At times, obedience to conscience requires departure. Moses fled Egypt, not out of fear alone, but because the hour for deliverance had not yet come. Joseph and Mary fled to Egypt with the Christ Child to preserve the promise until it could stand in the open. To flee is not cowardice when its purpose is preservation. It is wisdom under threat—obedience in retreat.

The church has often survived by flight. The faithful hid in deserts and catacombs, not to escape obedience but to preserve it. What appears as weakness to the world may be strategy in the kingdom. There are moments when silence guards truth and withdrawal protects witness for a later hour.

2. TO DISOBEY YET SUBMIT— THE PATH OF WITNESS

There are times when escape is impossible and the command of man stands in open conflict with the command of God. In such moments, the believer must obey heaven. Yet even in defiance, he remains submissive in spirit. Daniel prayed knowing the cost. The Hebrew exiles refused to bow but spoke with respect. Their disobedience was without rebellion; their submission was without surrender.

This is the purest test of conscience. It separates conviction from pride and courage from anger. When Peter and John told the Sanhedrin, "We must obey God rather than men," they did not speak with hatred. They broke human command but upheld divine order.

To disobey yet submit is to bear the cross in public view. It refuses falsehood yet accepts the suffering that follows. The believer who walks this path exposes tyranny not by force but by endurance. He allows injustice to condemn itself against the light of righteousness and trusts that truth, once lifted, will draw men toward God.

3. TO FAITHFULLY RESIST—THE PATH OF RENEWAL

There is a third calling—the most demanding of all. When evil seeks not only to silence truth but to destroy the innocent, conscience may require active opposition. This is faithful resistance: action measured by law, governed by love, and restrained by humility.

Faithful resistance is not rebellion. It is obedience in motion. It confronts not to seize power but to protect life. When Moses faced Pharaoh, when Esther confronted Haman, when prophets rebuked kings, they resisted not out of defiance but devotion. They defended the holy purpose of authority against its corruption.

The faithful do not reject authority; they refuse its perversion. They remember that authority itself is sacred, and that to restore it is an act of loyalty, not revolt. The prophet's rebuke is not contempt for the throne but intercession for its redemption.

Through every age, the church has walked these paths—fleeing under Nero, disobeying under Diocletian during the Great Persecution, resisting under kings who claimed to rule for God while denying him in deed. Her strength has never been in number but in conscience. Every revival of liberty began with the return of moral clarity. From Exodus to Reformation, from hidden churches to public witness, the pattern remains: obedience to God is the foundation of every just society.

Measured resistance is not an event but a disposition. It lives ready. It neither seeks conflict nor fears it. It knows when to withdraw, when to endure, and when to stand. It carries the cross in one hand and the sword of truth in the other—praying that the latter need never be drawn.

The day may come when each believer must choose one of these paths. When it comes, courage will depend not on circumstance but on formation. A conscience trained by Scripture and tested by suffering will know its way. It will not ask permission to obey God.

And when it acts—whether in silence, in defiance, or in defense—it will do so with the same spirit that marked its Lord: meekness without fear, strength without pride, and truth without compromise.

CALL TO FAITHFUL RESISTANCE—THE TRIAD OF COURAGE

When authority commands what God forbids, will you flee, disobey, or stand? Each path requires humility before it demands courage. The test is not whether you prevail, but whether you remain faithful when victory costs you everything.

To resist rightly is to love purely—courage without hatred, conviction without pride, and truth without fear.

> Acts 5:29—"Peter and the other apostles replied: 'We must obey God rather than human beings!'"

Obey God even when obedience costs peace. Resist sin without hatred. Disobey false commands with humility. Stand firm when silence serves evil. Let your courage reveal whom you fear.

The apostles showed how truth stands before power; the early fathers showed how it suffers under it. They carried the same conscience-bound courage into courts, arenas, and tribunals. Their witness forms the backbone of faithful resistance: peaceful, truthful, and unbreakable.

CHAPTER 8

The Doctrine of Conscience

Rom 2:15—"They show that the requirements of the law are written on their hearts, their consciences also bearing witness, and their thoughts sometimes accusing them and at other times even defending them."

Conscience is the first sanctuary and the last court. It existed before temple or tabernacle, before priest or law. It is the echo of God's voice left in man after Eden—the inward law that bears witness to the outward one. To understand conscience is to understand the mystery of human freedom under divine authority.

The apostle Paul saw this clearly. When he wrote that the law is "written on their hearts," he was describing revelation, not emotion. Conscience is the living tablet of divine order. It does not invent truth; it recognizes it. It is not the source of morality but the seat of its awareness. Even among those without Scripture, conscience testifies that there is a Judge above man and a law that cannot be repealed.

THE NATURE OF CONSCIENCE

Conscience is not memory; it is participation in divine judgment. It is the faculty by which the soul aligns with righteousness or recoils from sin. It can be dulled, silenced, or seared—but never erased. Like the pilot light of the spirit, it may flicker, yet it does not die. Every person, believer or not, carries an imprint of moral awareness that points back to its Maker.

When conscience is pure, it harmonizes the inner man with God's law. When defiled, it distorts perception itself. A dulled conscience cannot tell mercy from compromise or justice from cruelty. Civilizations do not collapse because they forget right and wrong; they collapse because they stop caring. It is not the absence of law that corrupts a nation, but the dulling of its shared conscience—the moral blindness of a people who once knew the difference and ceased to defend it.

THE FORMATION OF CONSCIENCE

If conscience is divine in origin, it must be divine in formation. It cannot be trained by public opinion or ruled by emotion. Only the Word of God refines it. Scripture does not give new morals; it restores old ones to clarity. Prayer purifies conscience through surrender; suffering sharpens it through testing. When disciplined by truth, conscience becomes the lamp of liberty—lighting both the inner life and the public square.

For the believer, conscience must be informed by revelation and confirmed by obedience. Knowledge without submission breeds arrogance; emotion without discernment breeds deception. The heart must feel what the mind knows, and both must bow before the Spirit of Truth.

When individual conscience is rightly ordered, the conscience of nations can also be renewed. No society rises above the souls that compose it.

THE ROLE OF CONSCIENCE IN AUTHORITY

A ruler without conscience becomes tyranny; a subject without conscience becomes slavery. True freedom is not the absence of law but the alignment of will with righteousness. The magistrate must govern by principle, not preference. The citizen must obey by conviction, not convenience. This is heaven's balance reflected on earth.

The early church understood this. When believers confessed, "Jesus is Lord," they made more than a statement of faith—they drew a boundary. That confession placed every other claim to lordship under judgment. Caesar might command taxes, but not worship. Conscience bowed to God alone. From that submission came the foundation of liberty itself, for where the Spirit of the Lord is, there is freedom (2 Cor 3:17).

THE WOUNDING OF CONSCIENCE

Though divine in origin, conscience is fragile in stewardship. It can be dulled by indulgence, hardened by pride, or manipulated by fear. The enemy's first victory is not deception but desensitization. He does not need to destroy truth if he can deaden the heart that hears it.

The greatest threat to the church is not persecution from without but anesthesia within—the slow numbing of moral perception. When believers excuse small evils for comfort's sake, they prepare their souls for greater compromise.

A nation's conscience dies the same way: quietly, beneath applause and legislation that trades truth for ease. When evil is normalized and good becomes suspect, the shared conscience has been seared. Only repentance can restore its life.

THE RESTORATION OF CONSCIENCE

But the God who wrote the law on the heart can also heal the heart that forgot the law. The Spirit convicts not to condemn but to cleanse. He awakens moral memory and renews the joy of obedience. This is regeneration—the conscience reborn, not rewritten.

Christ, who bore the penalty of the broken law, restores the harmony of the soul. His blood speaks better things than that of Abel (Heb 12:24)—not vengeance, but vindication. It cleanses even the guilty conscience, turning judgment into joy and the heart into a sanctuary again.

THE CONSCIENCE AS THE LAMP OF LIBERTY

When the church teaches, she forms conscience. When she prays, she polishes its lens. When she suffers faithfully, she keeps its flame alive before a darkened world. The believer's conscience, rightly formed, becomes a lighthouse to the age—reminding kings and commoners alike that no law outranks the law of God.

So long as conscience remains alive, hope remains possible. Tyrants fear it more than armies, for it cannot be silenced by decree. It is the remnant of Sinai within the soul—the law still alive in flesh and blood, declaring even in prison or exile that truth is free.

Conscience is not a side study of theology; it is the engine of history. It builds nations and brings them to judgment. When rightly ordered, it speaks for God within man. When corrupted, it imitates God in man's own voice. The future of nations depends on which voice they obey—the echo of Eden or the Word of the living God.

CALL TO FAITHFUL RESISTANCE—GUARD THE SANCTUARY WITHIN

The first battle of every believer is fought in silence—within the walls of the heart where only God and conscience converse. There the soul decides whether truth will remain enthroned or be exiled for convenience. To guard this inner sanctuary is to preserve the kingdom of God within the self.

Faithful resistance does not begin with protest but with purity. A man who governs his thoughts has already conquered the world that tempts him. A conscience kept clean becomes a fortress against deception and a lamp against despair.

Let the faithful therefore tend their hearts as priests tend the altar. The fire of holiness, once neglected, soon dies; but when nourished with humility and truth, it illumines not only the soul but the age around it.

Guard the sanctuary within, for there sits the throne of God in miniature—and upon its purity depends the light of nations. When that inner flame burns clear, darkness cannot stand, and the disciple whom Jesus loved becomes its proof.

> Gal 5:13—"You, my brothers and sisters, were called to be free. But do not use your freedom to indulge the flesh; rather, serve one another humbly in love."

Use freedom for service, not for self. Defend liberty by living responsibly. Resist any freedom that corrupts others. Let your choices honor the One who freed you. Keep liberty bound to love.

CHAPTER 9

The Witness of John: Light, Truth, and Resistance

John 1:5—"The light shines in the darkness,
and the darkness has not overcome it."

"The light does not argue with darkness; it reveals it."
—*Faithful Resistance*, ch. 9

If conscience is the first sanctuary, as we have seen, John shows us the Light that fills it—the Word who enters the darkness and teaches the heart to see. From the first line of his Gospel, John writes as the theologian of conscience—translating revelation into moral sight. He begins not with the manger but with eternity: "In the beginning was the Word." In that Word was life, and that life was the light of all mankind. For John, salvation is illumination—light entering darkness, truth confronting deceit, conscience awakening from death.

The law commanded. The prophets warned. But John revealed. He opened the eyes of the soul to see that the Light has always been shining. Every act of repentance, every cry for justice, every awakening of moral awareness reflects that same eternal Light—the One who "gives light to everyone coming into the world" (John 1:9).

THE LIGHT THAT REVEALS

Light does not argue with darkness; it exposes it. Truth wins not by force but by clarity. The same command that shaped creation shapes conscience: "Let there be light." Where light enters, separation follows. The soul begins to discern. The church begins to repent. The nation begins to judge.

John records this separation in every confrontation of Christ's ministry. When Jesus spoke to the Pharisees, their blindness was revealed not by his condemnation but by their reaction. "This is the verdict," John writes: "Light has come into the world, but people loved darkness instead of light because their deeds were evil" (John 3:19).

The test of every age remains the same: what a man does with truth reveals what he loves.

Revelation is not a privilege reserved for a spiritual few; it is the universal gift of God. Scripture presents light as the inheritance of every person, the illumination that awakens conscience and calls the soul to return. God does not create spiritual castes. He speaks to all, teaches all, and summons all through the same light that exposes the truth of every heart. Whenever revelation is treated as something given to some but withheld from others, the truth has already been distorted. The moment spiritual knowledge becomes the possession of an inner circle, the witness of John has been exchanged for the whisper of Eden, where the serpent first promised a special enlightenment denied to others.

Hardening is not a divine exclusion but the moral consequence of resisting the light God gives. When truth is received, conscience becomes clear; when truth is resisted, conscience grows dull. Scripture presents this pattern as relational: the soul turns from the truth, the heart stiffens, and God confirms the posture the person has chosen. Hardening is woven into the created order—the spiritual physics of a moral universe—and its purpose is not destruction but revelation. By allowing the consequences of sin to ripen, God exposes their emptiness so that repentance may become possible.

False revelation always grows from the soil of elitism. The belief that some are born into spiritual advantage while others are born into spiritual impossibility is the oldest lie in the world. True revelation calls every soul to repentance and holds every conscience accountable to the same light. God's word does not divide humanity into separate destinies; it reveals humanity in its shared need. When the light shines, it shines upon all. When the truth speaks, it speaks to all. The gospel is universal not because all believe, but because all are addressed. And judgment is just precisely because no one is left without the light that God has given.

One of the great errors of our age, and of many ages before it, is the failure to distinguish the God who inhabits eternity from the creatures who inhabit time. When we imagine the Father deliberating, reacting, or choosing the way we do, we commit a simple but destructive category error—attributing the properties of time to the One who stands outside of it. Jesus confronted this confusion directly in John 6. "No one can come to me unless the Father who sent me draws him," he said; yet in the next breath he added, "Everyone who listens to the Father and learns from him comes to me." The drawing is eternal; the coming is temporal. The Father illumines; the believer responds. When the categories remain distinct, sovereignty and responsibility walk in harmony. When they collapse, conscience collapses with them. The God who orders the universe does not coerce the soul; he enlightens it. And the soul, awakened by his teaching, becomes capable of the faithful resistance history demands.

THE TRUTH THAT CONFRONTS

In John's Gospel, truth is not a concept but a Presence. "I am the way, the truth, and the life" (John 14:6). Truth is not an argument to be won but a Person to be obeyed. The church's calling is not to defend truth as if it were fragile, but to live it as if it were final.

This is the resistance of light: truth refusing disguise. It does not dim itself to gain acceptance; it shines because it must. Christ's miracles were acts of mercy; his words were acts of war—light dividing falsehood from faith. Before Pilate, he spoke not as defendant but as Judge: "Everyone on the side of truth listens to Me" (John 18:37).

Pilate's question—"What is truth?"—was not inquiry but evasion, the weapon of every tyrant: to make truth seem uncertain so that power may seem necessary. Yet as he spoke, Truth stood before him—silent, unyielding, sovereign.

THE RESISTANCE THAT REDEEMS

John shows that resistance begins not with defiance but with abiding. "If you hold to My teaching," Jesus said, "you are really My disciples. Then you will know the truth, and the truth will set you free" (John 8:31–32). Freedom is the fruit of faithfulness, not rebellion. To abide is to resist corruption steadily, without surrender.

This was the power of the early church. They did not overthrow Rome; they outlived it. The empire ruled by fear; they endured by faith. Swords could break bodies, but not light. Every martyr who forgave his persecutor drove darkness back. Their mercy achieved what no sword could—it turned violence upon itself and exposed its emptiness. Every believer who spoke truth in love exposed the impotence of lies.

Resistance, in John's vision, is revelation. When conscience stands firm, the Light unmasks the shadow, and evil condemns itself by its reaction. The church that abides in truth becomes the lampstand of God (Rev 2:5)—not brilliant by its own merit, but radiant by the flame entrusted to it.

THE CONSCIENCE THAT BEARS WITNESS

For John, revelation ends in testimony. "This is the disciple who testifies to these things" (John 21:24). Truth is fulfilled when it is spoken. The same Spirit who illuminated John now commands every believer to bear witness—not only in word but in moral clarity.

The world does not hate the church because she does evil, but because she exposes it. Light is intolerable to eyes accustomed to darkness. Yet even persecution becomes proof that the church still shines. When truth provokes hostility, it proves its purity. When conscience suffers for righteousness, it participates in the cross.

THE VICTORY THAT IS ALREADY WON

John ends where he began—not with fear, but with assurance. The darkness has not overcome the light. Every act of conscience—every quiet refusal of corruption, every defense of the innocent, every confession of truth—shares in that eternal victory.

The world may appear powerful, but its shadow is temporary. The Word remains. The Light that shattered the tomb now burns within the redeemed. No empire, ideology, or decree can extinguish it. The conscience kindled by Christ is the ember of eternity within time. To guard it is to keep creation aligned with its Creator.

Thus, gospel's fulfillment completes the divine pattern:

- The law revealed God's righteousness.
- The cross revealed God's mercy.
- The Light reveals God's truth in every conscience awakened by grace.

And when the world rages against that Light, the faithful answer not with fury but with faith: "The darkness has not overcome it."

REFLECTION: THE FIRST LIE AND THE OLD ERROR

The first heresy did not arise in a distant century but in the first garden. The serpent did not tempt Eve with rebellion alone but with elevation: "You will be like God." It was the promise of spiritual advantage—a knowledge beyond the reach of others. That moment planted the seed of spiritual elitism, the belief that some stand nearer to God by nature while others never can. Gnosticism simply repeated this lie in philosophical form. It divided humanity into two fixed classes—those with a hidden divine spark and those without hope of ever receiving it. Salvation, in that system, was not the call to conscience but the privilege of an inner circle.

The apostles rejected this vision because it contradicted everything Christ revealed. Scripture presents light as God's gift to all—the illumination that awakens every conscience and summons every soul to repentance. Whenever revelation is treated as privilege rather than invitation, the shadow of Eden returns. And every age has found new ways to dress that shadow in religious language. But the light of Christ breaks it by declaring that no one is born beyond reach, no one is excluded from the summons, and no one stands outside the dignity of being called. Revelation does not create spiritual elites; it reveals spiritual need. And the God who speaks to all will judge all by the light he has given.

CALL TO FAITHFUL RESISTANCE—SHINE WITHOUT PRIDE, SHINE WITHOUT FEAR

The light of Christ exposes every false hierarchy. Revelation is not the secret property of the spiritual elite but the inheritance of every person created in the image of God. To walk in the light is to renounce every form of superiority—whether intellectual, spiritual, or doctrinal. Pride darkens; humility illuminates. Faithful resistance requires both: to shine without arrogance and to expose darkness without cruelty.

Do not believe the lie that revelation is reserved for the few. Do not accept any teaching that treats salvation as selective rather than universal in its summons. Let your conscience stand under the same light that addresses all humanity. Resist every voice—religious or secular—that claims access denied to others. The darkness fears the light because light levels the field: all are seen, and all are called. Do not dim the light for acceptance or hide it for safety. The darkness has not overcome it—and it will not. Your faithfulness exposes falsehood more powerfully than argument. What you refuse to become is as much a testimony as what you boldly proclaim.

> Eph 5:11—"Have nothing to do with the fruitless deeds of darkness, but rather expose them."

Expose what is false with courage and humility. Shine in such a way that others see Christ's light, not the shadow of yourself. For the Light triumphs not by force but by faithfulness—and the darkness has not overcome it.

CHAPTER 10

The Law of Sin and God's Law

Rom 7:22–23—"For in my inner being I delight in God's law; but I see another law at work in me, waging war against the law of my mind and making me a prisoner of the law of sin at work within me."

"The cross conquers what the sword can only restrain."
—*Faithful Resistance*, ch. 10

If John reveals how the Light awakens conscience, Paul reveals the war that conscience enters—the conflict between the law of God and the law of sin. The greatest battlefield in history is not the plain of nations but the chambers of the human heart. Before swords are drawn or decrees written, the war begins within. Paul called it the conflict between the law of God and the law of sin—two powers contending for one conscience, two governments vying for one soul.

This struggle is not merely moral but spiritual. The law of God reveals righteousness; the law of sin rebels against it. Both claim authority, but only one grants freedom. Humanity's tragedy is not ignorance of good but bondage to it—knowing truth yet failing to keep it, seeing light yet preferring shadow. Conscience, caught between revelation and corruption, becomes both judge and prisoner.

THE LAW THAT CONDEMNS AND THE LAW THAT LIBERATES

The Mosaic law was perfect in holiness but powerless to transform. It revealed sin but could not remove it. Like a mirror, it exposed the stain but offered no cleansing. Its purpose was diagnostic, not curative—to awaken conscience and prepare it for grace. When Paul cried, "Who will rescue me from this body of death?" he spoke for all humanity. The law had done its work: it exposed the disease so the soul might seek the Physician.

Christ is that Physician. He fulfilled the law not by lowering its demand but by embodying its perfection. The righteousness once commanded is now imparted by grace. The believer is freed not from the law but through it—through its fulfillment in Christ's obedience. The law remains holy, but it is now written on hearts renewed by the Spirit.

Where the Spirit reigns, sin loses dominion. The old nature still resists but no longer rules. The heart once enslaved becomes a sanctuary of divine order. The law that condemned now instructs; the command that exposed now empowers. Grace does not erase the moral law—it engraves it deeper until obedience becomes delight.

THE CONSCIENCE AS BATTLEFIELD

Every believer lives between these two laws. The mind delights in truth, but the flesh rebels. Paul himself confessed, "I do not do the good I want to do, but the evil I do not want to do—this I keep on doing" (Rom 7:19). This struggle is not failure; it is faith alive. Only a living conscience can feel conflict. The dead are at peace with their chains; only the free wrestle against them.

This warfare is the training ground of faithful resistance. Before a man can stand against tyranny in the world, he must overcome the tyranny within. Self-rule under God is the foundation of all moral authority. A man who will not govern himself by truth cannot help govern others by justice.

The conscience must learn to discern between conviction and accusation—between the Spirit's correction and the enemy's condemnation. One restores; the other destroys. The Spirit convicts to cleanse, never to crush.

The battle within is real, not symbolic. Paul reminds us that "our struggle is not against flesh and blood, but against rulers, authorities, and powers of this dark world" (Eph 6:12). The unseen realm governs the visible; spiritual order shapes civil order. When the believer resists sin, he joins the same conflict waged in heaven's courts. The armor of God—truth, righteousness, faith, and the word—is not metaphor but armament. Conscience becomes both fortress and front line, where invisible loyalties are declared.

Faithful resistance begins in the soul but echoes through creation. Victory within precedes renewal without.

THE LAW WRITTEN ON THE HEART

The new covenant does not relax the law; it relocates it. "I will put my laws in their minds and write them on their hearts," says the Lord (Heb 8:10). The same hand that wrote on stone now inscribes on flesh. What once required enforcement now flows from affection. Obedience becomes joy because love has replaced fear as the soul's motive.

This is regeneration—compulsion transformed into communion. The believer obeys not to earn favor but to express it. Holiness becomes harmony: the resonance of conscience with divine will. The heart that once resisted now rejoices; what was duty becomes delight.

SIN'S COUNTERFEIT LAW

Even dethroned, sin deceives. It mimics righteousness with counterfeit morality. It flatters emotion as truth and confuses preference with conscience. This is freedom corrupted—when man becomes his own measure of good.

A conscience detached from Scripture is a compass without north. It moves, but it misleads. An age that trusts its moral instincts will soon sanctify its vices. The only safeguard is the indwelling Word—the written law illuminated by the living Spirit. Only when conscience submits to that light can freedom endure.

THE VICTORY OF GRACE

The war between sin and law ends not in despair but in deliverance. "Thanks be to God, who delivers me through Jesus Christ our Lord!" (Rom 7:25). Grace does not silence the law; it fulfills it. The believer no longer stands accused but stands aligned. The command that condemned now becomes song.

The conscience once at war becomes the throne of peace. Sin remains as noise but not as ruler. The government of grace within the heart begins to heal the government of man. A people ruled by conscience will rule justly; a people ruled by appetite will consume themselves. The health of nations depends on the holiness of hearts.

As long as sin's law rages, faithful resistance remains. But that resistance begins within. The cross has disarmed the accuser and enthroned conscience under Christ. The battle continues, but victory is certain: "The law of the Spirit of life has set you free from the law of sin and death" (Rom 8:2).

THE LAW AND THE POLIS

The Christian lives between two sovereignties—the kingdom eternal and the city temporal. He is citizen of both, servant of one. The *polis*—the ordered community of human law—is not heaven's rival but its proving ground. The very word *politics* is born of *polis*, the gathering of citizens pursuing the common good. But through time, politics drifted from purpose. What began as truth seeking became power keeping.

The Law of Sin and God's Law

Many believers, weary of corruption, now flee the public square. Yet in doing so, they abandon the moral field to those who worship power instead of truth. Withdrawal is not holiness when it abdicates responsibility. The conscience formed by Christ must engage the polis—not as partisan, but as witness; not to conquer, but to consecrate.

Law, rightly ordered, is mercy structured for the common good. But when law forgets its Maker, it becomes rebellion disguised as order. To honor government is obedience; to worship it is idolatry. The disciple must therefore learn holy engagement—to serve within the city without surrendering the kingdom, to speak truth in the forum without forfeiting faith.

The Christian renders to Caesar what is Caesar's but never the conscience that is God's. He serves, prays, and speaks under authority but never under fear. His allegiance is sealed not by policy but by baptism. His public life exists to preserve conscience in the midst of coercion. Truth, not force, is the foundation of every just society.

When the church trades the cross for the scepter, she ceases to witness and begins to rule—and ruling, she falls. The sword restrains evil, but only the Spirit renews the heart. And yet many well-intentioned people, including Christians, forget what the sword actually is. Every law, however noble in intent, is ultimately enforced by coercion. Government does not persuade; it compels. The state can restrain injustice, but it cannot create righteousness. When believers look first to legislation to accomplish what only the Spirit can produce, they unintentionally substitute force for faith and policy for discipleship. Good ends do not sanctify coercive means. What the sword enforces externally, only truth can form internally.

The kingdom of God advances not by legislation but by light—truth lived, spoken, and endured until hearts yield freely to Christ.

Many confusions about authority—both sacred and civic—come from a deeper confusion about God himself. When we drag the Father into the sequence of time, imagining him choosing, adjusting, or responding as rulers do, we collapse the eternal into the temporal and lose the boundary that protects both conscience and kingdom. Jesus kept these realms clear: "They will all be taught by God," and, "Everyone who listens to the Father and learns from him comes to Me" (John 6:45, quoting Isa 54:13). The Father governs by illumination, not intervention. His authority awakens; it does not coerce. The state may restrain with the sword, but God rules by truth. And truth persuades only when the conscience remains free under his teaching. When the Father's eternal work is confused with the magistrate's temporal work, the church excuses tyranny and the state claims divinity.

And whenever the heart elevates itself above others, the error does not remain private. The spiritual elitism John exposes becomes the blueprint for every worldview that exalts a few above the many. What begins as a claim to special insight—whether philosophical, political, or religious—soon ripens into the right to rule, manage, or coerce. *Elitism hardened inward becomes domination outward.* The moment a man believes he sees what others cannot, he soon believes he may control what others must.

Faithful resistance begins by keeping the categories straight: the Father enlightens eternally, the Son redeems historically, and the conscience obeys freely in the light of both.

Once the eternal work of the Father and the redemptive work of the Son are kept clear, the story of faithful resistance becomes unmistakable. Every age repeats the same pattern: truth is revealed, power resists it, and God multiplies what the world tries to destroy. The conscience, once anchored in the Word, becomes the most dangerous force to any kingdom built on fear.

JOHN 12:23—"THE HOUR HAS COME FOR THE SON OF MAN TO BE GLORIFIED."

The Roman Empire believed that truth could be silenced by force. But the early church learned that truth under pressure does not weaken—it multiplies. No writer saw this more clearly than Tertullian, the fiery lawyer-theologian of the second century. In *The*

Apology, his defense of the Christian faith before the Roman governors, he made a declaration that outlived the Empire itself: "The oftener we are mown down by you, the more in number we grow; the blood of Christians is seed" (*Apology* 50.13).

Tertullian was not offering poetry. He was describing a law of the kingdom as real as gravity: persecution planted the very seeds that persecution attempted to destroy. Rome scattered blood; God gathered a harvest.

Jesus had already taught this long before Tertullian wrote his defiant line. Standing in Jerusalem during the final week of his ministry, he declared, "The hour has come for the Son of Man to be glorified" (John 12:23). Then he revealed the hidden order beneath all faithful resistance: "Unless a grain of wheat falls to the ground and dies, it remains alone. But if it dies, it produces many seeds" (John 12:24).

The kingdoms of this world assume that crushing a witness ends his influence. Christ reveals the opposite—death in obedience becomes multiplication in power. The sword can destroy the body, but only God can determine the harvest.

This has always been the pattern. Whenever rulers strike at the conscience of the faithful, the witness of those who bow only to Christ becomes the seed of renewal for others. The empire sees loss; heaven sees planting. This is why every generation must recover the courage to stand, for the fruit borne tomorrow depends upon the faithfulness sown today.

This is also why the dedication of this book matters. Faithful conviction, when tested, becomes seed. Those who stand publicly for truth—whether in Rome or in the modern public square—pay a price. But God wastes nothing. The witness of conscience becomes the seed of courage in others. The harvest belongs to him.

LUTHER BEFORE THE EMPIRE

In the long contest between truth and power, conscience must sometimes stand alone. In 1521, Martin Luther stood before Emperor Charles V at the Diet of Worms. His writings—*The*

Ninety-Five Theses, On the Babylonian Captivity of the Church, and *The Freedom of a Christian*—had shaken Europe by declaring salvation through faith, not indulgence or decree.

Pressed to recant, he answered with the confession that defines faithful resistance:

> Unless I am convinced by the testimony of the Scriptures or by clear reason . . . my conscience is captive to the Word of God. I cannot and will not recant anything, for it is neither safe nor right to go against conscience. Here I stand, I can do no other. God help me. Amen.[1]

He spoke not as rebel but servant—a man who knew that conscience bound to truth is higher than authority bound to error. The court could threaten his life but not command his soul. Conscience anchored in Scripture stands beyond decree.

Declared an outlaw, Luther hid in Wartburg Castle, translating the New Testament into German so that every soul might hear the word in its own tongue. The Reformation began not with revolt but with obedience—the obedience of a conscience unwilling to betray its Lord.

The Diet of Worms became a monument to that truth: that conscience bound to God's word is the truest seat of freedom under heaven.

The state may command allegiance, but conscience renders worship. The believer serves within the polis as witness, not ward—as salt that preserves, not power that dominates. He seeks the peace of the city not by compromise but by conversion, building its welfare through righteousness. Thus the church fulfills her civic calling without surrendering her holy one.

The polis is the theater of obedience; politics is its distortion. To serve the first is duty; to be ruled by the second is deception. The believer stands where heaven meets earth—the conscience of the city, governed by a law older than nations and higher than kings.

---

1. Martin Luther, "Declaration at the Diet of Worms," in *Luther's Works*, vol. 32, ed. George W. Forell (Philadelphia: Fortress, 1958), 112–13.

The Law of Sin and God's Law

THE JOURNEY OF THE MAYFLOWER—FROM PERSECUTION TO COVENANT LIBERTY

> Heb 11:13–16—"They admitted that they were foreigners and strangers on earth. . . . They were longing for a better country—a heavenly one."

The story of *Faithful Resistance* continued across the sea. When conscience found no refuge in the courts of kings, it sailed for a shore still unseen. Those who made that passage were not adventurers seeking gain, but believers seeking freedom to obey God. They were Puritan Separatists—souls who refused to bow to a state-made church. Their journey from persecution to covenant liberty became the living pattern of truth preserved through exile.

Persecution in the Realm of Conformity

Late-sixteenth-century England demanded uniform worship. The crown ruled the conscience through bishops, and to question *The Book of Common Prayer* was to question the throne itself. Yet a remnant would not yield. They met in barns and fields, reading the word without license, praying without permission. Their pastors were hunted and hanged, but the people learned what cannot be silenced—that the true church is not an arm of the state but the gathered body of Christ under his authority alone. Every prison cell became a classroom in conscience. Their obedience deepened into principle: that God alone commands the soul.

Exile in Holland—Liberty Without Rest

In 1608 the Scrooby congregation escaped England, finding haven in Leiden. There they worshiped freely, yet freedom revealed its own trial. They labored as strangers, poor in wealth but rich in conviction. Their children began to absorb the customs of the Dutch, and the fathers feared that liberty without holiness would dissolve their faith. They discovered what all free peoples must learn: that liberty unguided by conscience decays into indulgence. So even in safety they longed again for pilgrimage—a place where faith could shape community under covenant, not under compromise.

The Voyage and the Covenant on the Sea

In 1620 they set sail. The *Mayflower* was no grand vessel, only a merchant ship heavy with hope. When storms drove them north of their chartered land, they faced a lawless coast and a divided crew. Before setting foot on shore, they bound themselves before God: "We . . . do solemnly and mutually, in the presence of God and one another, covenant and combine ourselves together into a civil body politic."[2]

This Mayflower Compact was not ambition—it was submission. They declared that just government arises from the moral consent of the governed under divine authority. On that fragile parchment, the conscience of a people took institutional form: self-government ordered by covenant before God.

Planting Plymouth—Covenant Made Flesh

Their first winter was famine and grave. Half died before spring. Yet the survivors did not curse their vow or flee their calling. They buried their dead by night so that enemies would not count their losses, and they prayed at dawn before finishing their shelters. Their endurance was worship. When spring broke, providence met them through Squanto—once enslaved, now returned—whose help sustained them. Their first harvest became a feast of thanksgiving, not conquest. They saw mercy where the world saw misfortune, and they gave thanks to the God who had led them through judgment into grace. From that soil a covenant people emerged, proving that

---

2. Mayflower Compact, in William Bradford, *Of Plymouth Plantation, 1620-1647*, ed. Samuel Eliot Morison (New York: Alfred A. Knopf, 1952), 75-76.

liberty without holiness is corruption, and holiness without liberty is bondage.

The Legacy of Conscience

From that frail colony grew the conviction that faith cannot be coerced and conscience cannot be owned. Later Separatists such as Roger Williams and William Penn would build whole commonwealths on that truth: that the state exists to restrain evil, but only God governs the soul. Their resistance was not rebellion; it was order reclaimed from corruption. Out of their suffering emerged the moral foundation of liberty—that government without God becomes tyranny, and faith without freedom becomes hypocrisy.

Patriotism rooted in gratitude, truth, and covenantal liberty is not nationalism; it is stewardship—the faithful care of the blessings God entrusts to a people.

Faithful Resistance Fulfilled

The Pilgrim story is not nostalgia but instruction. It teaches that conscience is the seed of every just nation and the altar of every true church. Their voyage was not an escape from duty but obedience carried forward by faith. They proved that truth, when lived, outlasts power. The liberty they sought was not license but law fulfilled in love—the freedom to obey God without fear. Their covenant still speaks: that a people bound to Christ will remain free, though the world binds them in chains.

Bridge to the Inner Kingdom

Thus the conscience that stood before the emperor crossed the sea with the exiles. The seat of Moses journeyed again—not in marble or crown, but in hearts that built by covenant what kings had tried to command by decree. Through persecution and passage the moral order endured, carried by a remnant who believed that divine authority could dwell among free men. And so the story of authority moved from the sword of empire to the soul of the believer, preparing the way for the law to be written once more upon the heart.

CALL TO FAITHFUL RESISTANCE—THE STEWARDSHIP OF CONSCIENCE IN THE CHURCH AND THE POLIS

The war between truth and deception is not only waged in the halls of power but in the house of faith. When conscience falls silent in the church, corruption takes the pulpit; when it falls silent in the city, corruption takes the law. Therefore, the faithful must keep watch in both sanctuaries—the altar and the assembly, the heart and the republic.

Christ did not redeem his people to withdrawal but to witness. The conscience shaped by grace must govern both soul and society. In the household of God, that stewardship begins with pastors and elders—shepherds charged to guard the flock, confront falsehood, and feed the people of truth. To tolerate deception for peace is to betray the very peace Christ purchased with his blood. The church must cleanse her lampstand before she can light the nation's path.

Yet the responsibility does not end at the altar. In a republic, the citizen is also steward; authority is shared trust. The polis itself is an extension of conscience—a moral field planted by God and maintained by his people. To abandon it is to surrender the seat of Moses to Pharaoh once more. Faithful resistance therefore demands engagement: reasoning without rage, voting without vanity, serving without compromise, standing without fear. Silence in the forum is disobedience in the soul.

But beware what happens when many speak and few think. Groups often do together what none would dare alone. The crowd excuses what the conscience condemns (Matt 27:22–23—"Crucify him!"). When men trade conviction for belonging, the voice of truth is drowned by the comfort of agreement. No gathering, however righteous in cause, can absolve the individual before God. Every believer must stand accountable for the words he repeats and the wrongs he permits, for the seat of judgment is single even when the crowd is many.

Engage the city not as partisan but as keeper of the seat—the citizen-priest who governs by conscience under Christ the King. In a government of the people, to neglect righteousness is to legislate decay. Hold leaders to justice, call neighbors to truth, and model the order you pray for. For a representative republic cannot remain free if its pulpits grow timid or its citizens indifferent.

Guard the flame of conscience within the church; extend its light into the polis. Let pastors teach the word without dilution, and let believers live the word without apology. The cross still governs every realm it touches. Christ is Lord of the altar and the assembly, of worship and of law.

Remember where resistance begins. The law is written on the heart before it shapes the polis; illumination precedes legislation; and every seed of courage is planted in secret long before it bears fruit in public. The state may restrain, but only the Spirit renews. When conscience bows to the Father's light, the believer becomes free from the fear that governs nations—and that freedom becomes the seed from which faithful resistance grows.

So stand your post—in prayer, in practice, in the public square. Keep the conscience clear and the covenant visible. Resist evil not with anger but with order, not with retreat but with righteousness; for when the church shines and the citizen stands, the lampstands are tended and the city remembers its light.

Movement III—The Seat Through History

"When conscience awakens, history moves."
—*Faithful Resistance*, ch. 11

CHAPTER 11

The Law of Redemptive Resistance: Conscience as the Seed of Renewal

Exod 1:17—"The midwives, however, feared God and did not do what the king of Egypt had told them to do; they let the boys live."

Every age of darkness has been answered by light. Every empire of coercion has been met by the quiet defiance of the faithful. When tyranny rises, God raises conscience to meet it. Redemptive resistance is not rebellion against authority; it is cooperation with grace. God confronts evil through the obedience of the few. History's deliverances are not accidents; they are moral awakenings.

From Scripture's first pages, resistance is woven into redemption. The Egyptian midwives feared God more than Pharaoh. Their courage was hidden, but its fruit was public: a people preserved and a deliverer spared. They disobeyed a king to obey a higher command. Redemption began not with power but with conscience.

Moses embodies this law. He was trained in empire yet schooled by conscience. His first attempt at deliverance was force without submission; his final act was obedience without force—standing before power with God's word and a staff. He did not overthrow Pharaoh's office; he appealed to its Origin.

THE PATTERN OF DIVINE INTERVENTION

God's method is consistent. When corruption hardens in power, he sends truth-tellers, not destroyers; reformers, not rebels. Elijah before Ahab, Nathan before David, John before Herod—each testified that authority is sacred only when submitted to God. Their words cut deeper than swords because they bore divine legitimacy.

Redemptive resistance clarifies covenant through conflict. Confrontation becomes a crucible: truth is defined, the faithful are tested, renewal begins. The Reformation, the abolition of slavery, and every moral reformation bear this imprint. Martyrs' blood, reformers' words, and the prayers of the persecuted are instruments of God's design.

Rome tolerated many religions, but only on one condition: every citizen must honor Caesar as supreme. Christians did not suffer because they worshiped Christ; they suffered because they refused to worship Caesar. Their loyalty to God alone looked like rebellion to an empire that demanded the conscience. This was not political sedition but spiritual fidelity—the first great witness that no ruler may claim what belongs to God.

THE MEASURE OF RESISTANCE

Not all resistance is redemptive. Motive draws the line. Holy defiance seeks righteousness; human rebellion seeks control. The measure is not the volume of protest but the purity of purpose. True resistance is ruled by love, or it becomes what it opposes. Its aim is faithfulness, not domination; deliverance, not victory for its own sake.

The cross is the measure. The most unjust act became salvation's means. Christ resisted not by force but by obedience unto death. His suffering turned violence into redemption. God does not merely permit conflict; he redeems it. Persecution purifies, oppression awakens courage, suffering exposes the vanity of power. The church grows in crisis more than in comfort, in persecution more than in privilege. Her strength is forged in resistance.

The Law of Redemptive Resistance

THE HARVEST OF CONSCIENCE

Every revival of faith follows moral confrontation. When conscience awakens, history moves. Exodus birthed covenant; the prophets prepared the Messiah's way; the Reformation recovered liberty of conscience; later awakenings rekindled nations' moral fire.

The pattern endures: corruption deepens, conscience awakens, resistance rises, redemption follows. This is the rhythm of divine renewal. Acts of faith—by prophet or peasant—become seeds of restoration. The law of redemptive resistance ensures evil never has the final word. What dies in obedience is raised in power.

THE ENDURANCE OF THE FAITHFUL

The cost is real. Redemptive resistance rarely draws applause. It invites misrepresentation, loss, and persecution. Yet in heaven's economy these losses are gain. Those who resist in truth participate in the redemption they proclaim. Endurance turns suffering into testimony.

Small acts endure: a prayer in a cell, a sermon before a hostile court, a letter from exile. Martyrs are not merely victims; they are victors whose obedience outlives their oppressors. Church history is this law in motion—from Rome's catacombs to Geneva's pulpits, from hidden churches to reformers before kings. Where men fear God more than rulers, history bends toward redemption.

THE FULFILLMENT OF THE PATTERN

The law of redemptive resistance will be fulfilled at Christ's return. The Lamb who resisted unto death will reign as the Lion who renews creation. The kingdoms of this world will become the kingdom of our Lord. Conscience will rest under perfect rule. Until then, the pattern continues: resistance as obedience, suffering as seed, victory as resurrection.

Every act that stands against evil hastens the day of righteousness. The midwives of Egypt, the prophets of Israel, the apostles of the cross—all testify that God works most powerfully through those who refuse unrighteousness even at highest cost. This law is not written in human statutes but engraved on redeemed hearts. Wherever it is honored, the kingdom advances by conscience, not conquest—by the obedience of saints, not the sword of men.

CALL TO FAITHFUL RESISTANCE—THE LAW OF REDEMPTIVE RESISTANCE

The history of redemption is written in acts of holy defiance. From Egypt's midwives to Rome's martyrs, conscience stood where compromise bowed. This law endures: every surrender to truth is a victory over evil. Stand in this lineage. Let your resistance become restoration. Let your obedience become revival.

> Rom 12:21—"Do not be overcome by evil, but overcome evil with good."

Fight injustice through holiness, not hatred. Let suffering refine, not embitter. Confront corruption by living differently. Return good for evil to expose evil's defeat.

The courage of the early martyrs did not vanish; it smoldered across the centuries until God ignited it again. When Scripture returned to the center and conscience was unbound by tradition, the pattern of faithful resistance reappeared in men like Luther. What the early church endured under Rome, the Reformers confronted in Christendom.

CHAPTER 12

The Failure of Church and State: When Conscience Became a Captive

Matt 22:21—"Render to Caesar what is Caesar's,
and to God what is God's."

"When the church crowns power, she abdicates truth."
—*Faithful Resistance*, ch. 12

The rise of Christendom began in triumph and ended in warning. What began as faith shaping power ended as power shaping faith.

Christendom was the long experiment in uniting faith and civilization—when the church's spiritual authority stood beside the state's political might, shaping law, culture, and conscience across nations. When the church left the catacombs for the courts of kings, she exchanged persecution for privilege. The cross, once a symbol of suffering love, became an ornament of empire. What began as the triumph of faith risked becoming the captivity of conscience.

The goal seemed noble: to harmonize heaven and earth. But the harmony was false. The eternal was placed beneath the temporal. The gospel's authority became entangled in the ambitions of men. When joined without humility, the state promised protection and the church offered legitimacy—a bargain that confuses stewardship with salvation. Together they built a monument of power, but its foundation was confusion—to whom does the soul belong? When power sanctifies itself, corruption becomes liturgy and no one dares call it sin.

THE MARRIAGE OF CONVENIENCE

When Constantine raised the cross above his armies, he did what emperors always do—he consecrated conquest. The church, weary of bloodshed, mistook peace for purity. In seeking safety, she surrendered sanctity. In gaining peace, she lost her prophetic voice. Baptism became citizenship. Conversion became currency. Faith multiplied in number but diminished in discernment.

Soon Caesar and church spoke the same language—kingdom, dominion, authority. The church adopted the vocabulary of empire; the empire borrowed the symbols of faith. What God had kept distinct—the conscience and the crown—was joined by convenience. The result was neither pure church nor just state, but a hybrid power incapable of repentance.

THE CORRUPTION OF AUTHORITY

When the state baptizes itself in God's name, it ceases to fear him. When the church takes the throne of kings, she forgets her power is moral, not coercive. Bishops became princes. Shepherds became magistrates. The seat of Moses was gilded in gold and guarded by soldiers.

The same empire that crucified Christ now crowned itself with his name. Heresy became treason. Dissent became rebellion. The kingdom of God became a bureaucracy of fear. The sword that once defended the innocent now silenced the faithful.

The conscience—once the church's crown—was chained in her dungeon. Men began to fear the priest more than the judge, the decree more than the gospel. The law that should have liberated souls was turned into bondage. What began as a kingdom of light dimmed beneath the shadow of its own success.

THE CRY OF THE PROPHETS

Yet even in corruption, conscience was not silent. God raised voices to remind both altar and throne that Christ's kingdom is not of this world. The true temple is built by devotion, not decree.

Through every century, reformers cried from within the system that betrayed them: "Render to Caesar what is Caesar's, and to God what is God's." They were not anarchists but intercessors—pleading for purity amid power.

Athanasius stood *contra mundum*—against the world—to defend the incarnation when councils and emperors bowed to convenience. Catherine of Siena rebuked popes with the authority of holiness, calling them from luxury to repentance. Wycliffe set the word loose in the language of the people, and Hus sealed that witness with fire rather than deny the truth he preached. Each bore what institutions could not: the conscience awakened by God against the corruption of his name. Together they form the ancient line of those who faced compromise with conviction and proved that truth needs no throne to endure.

Their suffering preserved what empire could not—the moral heart of the faith. Christendom faltered, but Christianity endured. The bride of Christ, stained yet unbroken, survived her captivity.

THE LESSONS OF HISTORY

The failure of church and state was not only political; it was theological. The kingdom of God cannot be legislated—only lived. When religion loses repentance, it gains ritual but loses reality. When faith becomes law, grace disappears. When religion becomes policy, repentance becomes irrelevant. A conscience forced rather than formed ceases to be conscience at all.

God never asked for alliance—only allegiance. The magistrate bears the sword to restrain; the church bears the cross to redeem. When these are exchanged, both lose their power. The sword cannot sanctify. The cross cannot coerce. The union of altar and throne produced conformity, not conviction—order without righteousness, ceremony without Spirit.

Yet even failure served grace. The long confusion of Christendom prepared the soil for renewal. Out of its ashes rose the cry for conscience. The Reformation, the rise of liberty, the separation of church and state—none rejected faith; they restored it to its rightful throne: the human heart.

THE RESTORATION OF CONSCIENCE

Christ's command still marks the boundary of moral order: "Render to Caesar what is Caesar's, and to God what is God's." The church may bless the state but must never become it. Her power is persuasion, not policy. Her authority is truth, not force.

When the church forgets this, she becomes an empire. When she remembers, she becomes a bride. Her strength lies not in dominion but devotion—not in decrees but in discernment. The world does not need a church that rules. It needs a church that reminds rulers of the law they cannot escape: the moral law written on every heart.

The lesson is clear: whenever the church weds the state, she becomes a widow within a generation. But when she weds Christ alone, she remains the mother of renewal.

So the faithful must guard the boundary with vigilance and humility. The conscience of nations depends upon the conscience of the church. Wherever that conscience remains clear, the throne of heaven still governs the affairs of men.

CALL TO FAITHFUL RESISTANCE—DO NOT WORSHIP THE UNION OF POWER AND PIETY

Every age builds its own golden calf—an altar to authority disguised as devotion. When church and state clasp hands without repentance, the beast stirs in miniature, and the false prophet blesses its banners.

Faithful resistance rejects this unholy alliance. The believer stands apart—not in rebellion but in reverence—bearing witness that no throne is holy but Christ's, and no law righteous that silences conscience.

> 1 Pet 2:17—"Show proper respect to everyone, love the family of believers, fear God, honor the emperor."

Distinguish reverence from worship. Respect rulers without surrendering conscience. Serve God before nation. Refuse alliances that corrupt holiness. Let loyalty be holy, not political.

But captivity gave birth to clarity; the conscience once chained to empire would soon break those bonds in the name of freedom under God.

History teaches us what happens when authority steps outside its lane. But Scripture teaches us why. Israel's seat of Moses was not a throne of domination but a seat of judgment under God's law. Before we confront the failures of later ages, we must return to the pattern God set from the beginning: authority under law, not above it.

CHAPTER 13

Conscience Under Creed: Lessons from Geneva

> Gal 5:1—"It is for freedom that Christ has set us free. Stand firm, then, and do not let yourselves be burdened again by a yoke of slavery."

> "Orthodoxy without mercy becomes tyranny in vestments."
> —*Faithful Resistance*, ch. 13

The Reformation began not in rebellion but in remembrance. It was conscience awakening after centuries of captivity beneath Christendom's crowns and councils. It was faith remembering its freedom and power relearning its limits.

The cry of reform was not liberty from faith but liberty for faith—a return to the authority of the Word and the freedom of the soul before God. Yet even this great renewal carried tension within it. The conscience that defied the corruption of Rome soon found itself confined by the rigor of its own success. Geneva became both the sanctuary of freedom and the warning of control.

Conscience Under Creed: Lessons from Geneva

THE AWAKENING OF CONSCIENCE

When Martin Luther stood before the Diet of Worms and declared, "My conscience is captive to the Word of God,"[1] the axis of authority shifted. Heaven's rule returned to the heart of man. The conscience, long buried under decrees, was restored to its throne beneath Christ.

The Reformers sought not chaos but clarity—to unchain the gospel from empire and return it to grace. John Calvin carried that work forward. In Geneva he envisioned a city governed not by tyranny but by truth, not by princes but by principle. His dream was covenant—a community where righteousness ordered every sphere of life. Yet in that dream lay peril: the pursuit of perfection can become its own master.

THE BURDEN OF THE PERFECT CITY

The Reformation freed conscience, but conscience under pressure seeks control. Geneva, refuge of Reformers, became a crucible of conformity. The Word that freed the soul was soon guarded by statute. Sermons became ordinances; confession became regulation.

Calvin did not intend tyranny; he feared its return. But in defending purity, the Reformers discovered how swiftly purity can become policy. When heresy was treated as crime, the sword once raised against Rome was turned inward. Servetus died under the same logic that once condemned the faithful. Zeal without mercy forged new chains. The conscience that cried, "Here I stand," stood upon another man's neck.

THE PARADOX OF LIBERTY AND LAW

Yet their failures must be seen in mercy. They were pioneers navigating moral wilderness. The Reformation restored liberty in principle, but not yet in practice. The world had not learned the

---

1. Martin Luther, *Defense and Explanation of All the Articles*, in *Luther's Works*, vol. 32, ed. George W. Forell (Philadelphia: Fortress, 1958), 112–13.

difference between governing by truth and governing for truth. The first preserves conscience; the second presumes upon it.

Calvin's Geneva gave the world both shadow and seed. Out of its tension grew the moral order of modern freedom—that law itself must answer to conscience and that faith must never be compelled. The theology that disciplined Geneva would, in time, discipline the nations. The same Scriptures once enforced by statute would later teach that enforcement cannot create belief.

THE REFINING OF THE REFORMATION

History refines its reformers. Their strengths become our warnings; their failures, our tutors. Geneva taught the church that orthodoxy without mercy becomes tyranny in vestments. Doctrine must be clothed in compassion or it condemns itself. Purity without humility freezes the faith it seeks to preserve. Whenever creed replaces charity, conscience grows cold.

The true legacy of the Reformation was not a perfect city but a purified gospel—salvation by grace alone, through faith alone, under Christ alone. That gospel, once freed from control, crossed oceans and continents. It planted seeds of conscience in every land. The free church and the free soul became the twin lights of Christian civilization.

THE LESSON FOR EVERY GENERATION

Each generation must guard the Reformation's gift from its shadow. Freedom, once secured, is always tempted to secure itself rather than to serve. Institutions preserve liberty only when they remain humbled before its Giver. Conscience, once exalted, tends toward pride. The church must remember that she is the bride, not the bridegroom—the voice of moral law, not its enforcer.

God alone governs the heart. The magistrate may restrain evil, but only the Spirit renews it. The reformer who forgets this becomes the ruler he once opposed. The pastor who turns creed into compulsion trades prophecy for policy. When faith must be forced, it ceases to be faith.

The lesson of Geneva endures: conscience must never be chained, not even by those who claim to guard it. The gospel that set Luther free must remain free. The liberty of the soul before God is sacred ground, and woe to those who violate it—whether through the coercion of rulers or the presumption of religion.

CALL TO FAITHFUL RESISTANCE—THE COURAGE OF CONVICTION

Creeds may describe faith, but only God defines it, and conscience bears its witness. Every generation must decide whether creed will serve truth or rule it. The church must hold the confession of hope without compulsion, and believers must bear witness with gentleness and resolve. Conviction is not arrogance; it is fidelity under fire—the courage to let truth remain free even when freedom costs everything. For it is written: "It is for freedom that Christ has set us free. Stand firm, then, and do not let yourselves be burdened again by a yoke of slavery" (Gal 5:1).

Freedom must be defended with vigilance, for history shows that not everyone who speaks of liberty preserves it. Creed must serve truth, never rule it. The faithful must resist control disguised as purity and challenge power that cloaks itself in doctrine. When faith is policed by fear, the conscience must still speak. For liberty is not preserved by silence but by steadfast souls who stand firm in the grace that makes all men free.

> Isa 33:22—"For the Lord is our judge, the Lord is our lawgiver, the Lord is our king; it is he who will save us."

The Reformation restored the dignity of conscience; the modern world attempted to build a civic order that protected it. Our constitutional structures did not emerge from political theory alone but from a long memory—Moses, Christ, the apostles, the martyrs, and the Reformers—converging on one truth: power must be restrained so conscience can remain free.

CHAPTER 14

Christ Among the Lampstands

Rev 1:13—"Among the lampstands was someone like a son of man, dressed in a robe reaching down to His feet and with a golden sash around His chest."

"Judgment begins not with the world, but with the worshiper."
—*Faithful Resistance*, ch. 14

The same Christ who once stood in the Court of the Gentiles now walks among the lampstands of his church. The same eyes that burned with zeal for his Father's house now search the hearts of his people. When he drove out the money changers, he was not cleansing a market but reclaiming a sanctuary. When he speaks to the seven churches, he does the same. The judgment that begins with the house of God is not destruction—it is renewal by fire.

The Revelation of John is not a riddle but a mirror of conscience. Before Christ unveils the seals of history, he examines those who bear his name. He walks among the lampstands not as a distant inspector but as the bridegroom whose bride has forgotten her first love. The light of the churches flickers, and he tends each flame, trimming the wicks and restoring the glow of holiness that alone can light the nations.

Every age must hear these letters again. They are not archives but oracles. The same temptations that shadowed Ephesus and

Pergamum shadow us still—pride of doctrine without devotion, comfort without conviction, tolerance that forgets truth, and wealth that dulls the Spirit. The lampstands have not changed; only the walls around them have.

Faithful resistance begins here—not with protest against the world but with repentance within the house of faith. The church cannot confront Caesar while serving Mammon, nor speak truth to power while flattering the powers within her own gates. Christ's first act of restoration is always purification. He overturns not the tables of strangers but the altars of self-interest erected in his name. Only when his house is clean does his light shine without shadow.

The church's warfare is not waged in the streets but in the spirit—though its fruits must still be lived in public through integrity and justice. When Christ walks among the lampstands, he moves through realms unseen, judging not flesh but faith. Each congregation is a spiritual outpost in invisible conflict. The principalities that tempt nations first whisper to churches, urging compromise where holiness once burned. Faithful resistance therefore requires vigilance on two fronts—the visible world of deeds and the invisible world of desires.

THE LETTERS TO THE CHURCHES

Ephesus—The Lost First Love

> Rev 2:4—"Yet I hold this against you: You have forsaken the love you had at first."

Christ honors Ephesus for labor, endurance, and discernment, yet his praise gives way to truth: "You have forsaken the love you had at first." They were right in word but wrong in spirit—orthodox yet cold, precise yet distant. In defending truth, they lost tenderness. His rebuke is an appeal of affection: remember, repent, and return. Faithful resistance cannot begin with indignation; it begins with devotion. Zeal without compassion becomes cruelty in righteous form. The church that forgets its first love turns vigilance into vanity. It is not protest but love that endures the night.

Pergamum and Thyatira—Power and Seduction

> Rev 2:14, 20—"You have people there who hold to the teaching of Balaam. . . . You tolerate that woman Jezebel, who calls herself a prophet."

If Ephesus erred in loveless orthodoxy, Pergamum and Thyatira erred in love without holiness. They welcomed the world in the name of grace and mistook tolerance for compassion. Pergamum blended worship and worldliness; Thyatira preached accommodation as wisdom. Both replaced consecration with compromise. These are not ancient errors but modern habits. The spirit of Balaam thrives wherever ministry becomes merchandise; the spirit of Jezebel rules wherever influence replaces integrity. Churches ally with power to gain protection, preachers soften truth to keep platforms, and disciples silence conscience to keep peace. Every compromise buys a smaller Christ.

Christ's words are surgical, not cruel. His sword proceeds from his mouth because only truth can heal deceit. The church's strength is not her influence but her innocence. To love the world is mission; to imitate it is death.

Sardis and Laodicea—The Appearance of Life

> Rev 3:1, 16—"You have a reputation of being alive, but you are dead. . . . So, because you are lukewarm—neither hot nor cold—I am about to spit you out of My mouth."

If Pergamum and Thyatira fell to compromise, Sardis and Laodicea fell to complacency. Their danger was not persecution but comfort—the corrosion that comes when faith costs nothing. Sardis had a name for life but was dead; Laodicea was rich and self-satisfied yet blind and poor. Their faith became tepid, their zeal measured by convenience.

Christ's voice is severe because his love is severe. He offers gold refined by fire and salve for their eyes. He stands at the door and knocks—not as a beggar but as a King reclaiming his house.

His remedy is not strategy but surrender. The church that opens the door finds fellowship restored: "I will come in and eat with them, and they with me" (Rev 3:20).

Smyrna and Philadelphia—The Faithful Remnant

> Rev 2:10, 3:8—"Be faithful, even to the point of death, and I will give you life as your victor's crown. . . . You have kept My word and have not denied My name."

Not all lampstands flickered. Amid fading light, two flames burned steady—Smyrna and Philadelphia. They were not powerful but persevering. In them Christ found no fault to rebuke, only faith to strengthen. Smyrna suffered and triumphed; Philadelphia endured and loved. Their endurance was their testimony. The measure of the church is not comfort but constancy. The persecuted and persevering have nothing left to protect but witness. In poverty they find purity; in weakness, strength. The faithful remnant becomes the bridge between purification and restoration—the conscience through which renewal begins.

THE CLEANSING AND THE CALL

> 1 Pet 4:17—"For it is time for judgment to begin with God's household."

Christ stands among his churches as Refiner, not accuser. His judgments are mercy in flame. The fire that purifies the altar in heaven cleanses the conscience on earth. Every rebuke is reclamation. He scours the temple not to destroy but to dwell.

Faithful resistance begins with purification. We cannot cry for justice in the streets while hiding injustice in the sanctuary. The same Christ who overturned the tables of commerce overturns the idols of comfort and success. His cleansing is preparation—a renewal of the lampstands so they may shine in a darkened age.

Let the shepherds of Christ's flock take up this charge first. Judgment begins with those who guard his word. To preach grace without repentance or to bless confusion as compassion is to dim the lamp entrusted to their care. The pulpit must recover its holy fire, that the pew may recover its holy fear. Renewal in the congregation will follow repentance in its leaders; holiness must burn at the altar before it spreads through the aisles.

In every generation he finds a remnant—a Smyrna that endures, a Philadelphia that holds fast. Their repentance becomes renewal; their tears become oil for the lamps. The faithful remnant becomes the conscience of the age—not by might but by the living presence of Christ within.

The vision ends not in despair but in dawn. The Lord who walks among his churches will one day gather them, purified and aflame, as the light of the new Jerusalem. Until that day, every act of faithful resistance begins where his fire still burns—in the heart cleansed by his word and consecrated to his love.

But a tended flame must become a guiding light. The church purified must become the church sent. When the lampstands burn pure, the city sees again what law alone could never reveal—the light of conscience made visible in community.

CALL TO FAITHFUL RESISTANCE—THE LAMPSTAND WITHIN

Let pastors remember that the saints they shepherd are a royal priesthood. Preach not to preserve attendance but to awaken allegiance. The church is not an audience but an army of light, each believer bearing the flame of witness. Faithful resistance must be taught, modeled, and preached—from pulpit to pew—until the conscience of the church burns again with holy fire.

Christ still walks among his lampstands, trimming wicks grown dim. Each heart is a sanctuary whose light must not fail; each believer, a steward of the flame. The test of the church is not survival but shine. Therefore, let every disciple tend the fire and carry it forth. *Resist the comfort of abstraction; let conviction take form in deed.* Confess what is dark, forgive what is broken, act where truth is silent. Let repentance become readiness, prayer become courage, holiness become witness. The world will not be illumined by anger but by endurance; not by outrage but by obedience.

Tend the flame—and lift it high. When the church burns pure, the nations see clearly; when her light returns, darkness retreats.

> Rev 3:19—"Those whom I love I rebuke and discipline. So be earnest and repent."

Begin reform at the altar, not the street. Repent before you resist. Clean the temple of your own heart first. Restore love before demanding change. Let repentance light your lamp.

Movement IV—The Restoration of Conscience

"The throne of God is restored first in the conscience of man."
—*Faithful Resistance*, ch. 15

CHAPTER 15

The Seat Within

> Jer 31:33—"I will put My law in their minds and write it on their hearts. I will be their God, and they will be My people."

What Christ restores among his lampstands, he now establishes within each soul. The authority purified in his church becomes personal in the conscience of every believer. The story of authority ends where it began—not in the thrones of men, but in the inner chamber of the soul. The true seat of Moses was never a chair in Jerusalem, nor a pulpit in Rome, nor a council table in Geneva. It was, and remains, the place where God communes with conscience. Every outward form of power—ceremonial, moral, or civic—exists only to serve this invisible throne within. When Christ fulfilled the law, he did not silence its moral voice; he internalized it. The commandments that once thundered from Sinai now whisper through the Spirit. "The kingdom of God is within you." Here, authority becomes intimacy—no longer imposed but indwelling; no longer external compulsion, but inward harmony. We enthrone our desires and call it discernment because true obedience would require surrender.

THE RETURN OF THE LAW TO THE HEART

The covenant that began in thunder continues in tenderness. The same God who engraved his word upon stone now inscribes it upon the softened heart. Conscience becomes the new Mount Sinai—trembling not with terror but with awe. The believer no longer ascends a mountain of smoke; he descends into a sanctuary of peace. In this inner kingdom, law and Spirit are not rivals but allies. The Spirit interprets what the law declares; the law confirms what the Spirit reveals. When both govern a man, he becomes whole. The divided self of Rom 7—"I do what I hate"—yields to the renewed mind of Rom 8—"The law of the Spirit of life sets you free from the law of sin and death." This is divine order restored: the throne of God reestablished in the conscience of man.

THE FREEDOM OF THE GOVERNED SOUL

Freedom, in the Christian sense, is not the absence of rule but the presence of righteousness. The liberated conscience is not lawless; it is rightly ordered. It submits to God not from fear but from love, and therefore resists tyranny without becoming rebellious. The soul ruled from within cannot be enslaved from without. This truth sustained prophets, apostles, and reformers alike. Their strength did not come from institutions but from conviction—the certainty that obedience to God outweighs every command of men. They stood unshaken because their seat of authority was immovable, anchored in the will of God.

THE CONSCIENCE AS ROYAL STEWARD

Every believer becomes royalty under Christ the King—royalty not of pride but of stewardship. Conscience is a borrowed throne, ruling only as it reflects the light of its Lord. When it exalts itself, it falls; when it submits, it reigns. This is the restoration of the moral priesthood—the believer as both subject and sanctuary. The tabernacle once built by hands now stands in living hearts. Worship is no longer ceremony but posture: the yielded conscience bowed before truth. Such souls become the moral infrastructure of nations. Laws on paper can restrain; laws on hearts can renew. When conscience governs the citizen, righteousness governs the land. When it fails, no constitution can save it.

THE SILENCE OF THE SEAT

The Seat Within is not loud. It does not thunder like kings or shout like crowds. It speaks in stillness: "Be still, and know that I am God." In that stillness, revelation descends. The world clamors for laws and revolutions, but heaven waits for listening souls. Here the faithful learn the difference between resistance and rebellion. The one rises from submission, the other from pride. The conscience that kneels before God stands rightly before men. It can endure injustice without hatred and love persecutors without compromise.

THE MIRROR OF ETERNITY

The Seat Within is also a mirror—a reflection of divine government. As conscience is cleansed, it begins to reflect God's image: justice balanced by mercy, strength tempered by humility. The believer becomes a microcosm of the kingdom. What God rules in heaven, he reproduces in the soul. This is the mystery Paul named "Christ in you, the hope of glory" (Col 1:27). The conscience, once defiled, becomes the dwelling of the King. The Spirit reigns where sin once ruled; peace sits where fear once trembled.

THE HARVEST OF THE INNER KINGDOM

When the law returns to the heart, the harvest of history begins. Humanity's soil—hardened by pride and power—is broken open by grace. Nations cannot repent until men do; institutions cannot reform until consciences awaken. Every true revival begins with the quiet reestablishment of this inner throne. This is the end toward which faithful resistance has always moved: not revolution, but restoration; not conquest, but communion. The law that once condemned now completes its purpose—it produces holy freedom. The believer ruled by Christ becomes the world's truest revolutionary: peaceful, principled, incorruptible. He fears no tyrant because he fears God alone. His allegiance is eternal, his loyalty unbought, his courage rooted in the indwelling Word.

THE THRONE RESTORED

Thus the story of the seat concludes where all authority began—in God's design for the soul. The kingdom of conscience is the foundation of every righteous order, the sanctuary of liberty, and the seed of every redemptive resistance. The world's thrones rise and fall, but the Seat Within endures. It is divine government in miniature, proof that heaven's authority can dwell in human form. And when Christ returns, that inward throne will be perfected, for "we shall be like him, for we shall see him as he is" (1 John 3:2). Until that day, every act of conscience—every quiet stand for truth, every refusal of deceit, every word of fidelity—builds the unseen kingdom. The law once carved in stone now lives in flesh, written by the Spirit upon the heart.

FAITHFUL RESISTANCE IN THE UNSEEN REALM

> Eph 6:12—"For our struggle is not against flesh and blood, but against the rulers, against the authorities, against the powers of this dark world and against the spiritual forces of evil in the heavenly realms."

The Seat Within stands amid a greater conflict—one that spans both the kingdoms of men and the realms unseen. The battle of conscience mirrors the warfare of heaven. The unseen realm is no abstraction; it is the deeper geography of history. What nations wage through power, souls wage through prayer. Every earthly tyranny begins as spiritual deceit; every act of faithfulness resounds in heaven. God's people have always fought on two fronts. Daniel's fasting in Babylon moved angels unseen (Dan 10); Elijah's prayer on Carmel shattered powers of darkness (1 Kgs 18:36–39). The prophets knew what modern man forgets—that principalities do not vanish because we ignore them. To deny them is not enlightenment but blindness.

Faithful resistance therefore requires discernment and devotion. The Spirit who gives courage before kings also grants sight within the spirit. The armor of God is not metaphor but the clothing of conscience for a war without cease: truth girds the mind, righteousness guards the heart, faith shields the soul, prayer breaks strongholds unseen. To resist in the spirit is to intercede in secret. The church that kneels in truth holds more power than armies that march without it. The visible world trembles under temporal thrones, but the unseen world moves by eternal decree. When the faithful stand, heaven stands with them. Thus every believer becomes both soldier and sanctuary—the conscience his post, the Spirit his commander, Christ his victory. To live in this awareness is to join the great resistance of holiness against corruption, of light against the long night of evil. Faithful resistance is never merely political or historical; it is spiritual. It begins where sight ends and endures where kingdoms fall. The unseen realm is real, and its battles are the truest reality of all.

CALL TO FAITHFUL RESISTANCE— THE SEAT WITHIN RESTORED

The final throne is not in heaven's distance but in the heart's dominion. Whoever rules there rules the life that follows. To enthrone Christ within is to unseat every rival—fear, pride, comfort, and compromise alike. Rise, then, not in defiance but in dominion under grace. Guard the inner throne with prayer. Govern your household by truth. Walk the world as one already ruled by heaven. Every just word, every merciful act, every refusal of deceit extends the reign of Christ through the conscience of his people. The world changes not when power shifts, but when hearts bow. When the Seat Within is reclaimed, every other throne is measured against it. This is the victory of the saints: the kingdom of God enthroned in the soul until it fills the earth.

> Ps 139:23-24—"Search me, God, and know my heart; test me and know my anxious thoughts. See if there is any offensive way in me, and lead me in the way everlasting."

Examine yourself before judging others. Keep your heart clear before keeping watch. Let conscience be renewed daily by truth. Surrender inner rule to Christ alone. Guard the throne within.

A system built to restrain power cannot endure if citizens abandon the virtues that restrain themselves. The crisis of our moment is not political first but moral: a people who no longer understand conscience will soon invite the very coercion they fear. Every failing republic begins with the failure of its inner life.

CHAPTER 16

The Faith of Faithful Resistance

Heb 11:1—"Now faith is confidence in what we hope for and assurance about what we do not see."

"Faith is the first resistance and the last."
—*Faithful Resistance*, ch. 16

Faithful resistance begins not with resolve but with faith in Jesus Christ. It is not the defiance of strong wills but the obedience of surrendered hearts. For only those who believe that Christ is Lord of both conscience and kingdom can resist evil without becoming it. Faith is not sentiment; it is sight restored—the soul's awakening to divine order. The early church spoke of faith as a living triad: *notitia, assensus, fiducia*—knowledge of Christ, assent to his truth, and active trust in his person. These three together form the ground of all faithful resistance. Without them, courage decays into pride; with them, obedience becomes worship.

From Adam's naming of Eve in hope of redemption to Abraham's belief in the God who provides, the story of faith has always been a story of divine trust against visible odds. The first act of faith was spoken in a fallen world—Adam calling his wife "Eve," the mother of all living, because he believed God's promise of new life through her. Abraham's faith raised the knife on Moriah and received back his son through the substitution of the Lamb. That same faith found its fulfillment at Calvary, where the Lamb of God bore sin and rose to new life. And that same faith will answer the final trumpet, when creation is made new and the race of faith is finished at last.

Faith is therefore not a single moment but a journey—a continual deepening of sight and surrender. It grows through knowledge (*notitia*), the increasing understanding of Christ through Scripture and Spirit. It matures through assent (*assensus*), the full agreement of the heart with what the mind has seen. And it finds completion in trust (*fiducia*), the lived obedience of one who believes that Christ's word is truer than circumstance. Together these movements form the rhythm of a faithful life: learning, believing, and acting in harmony with the will of God.

One of the great confusions of modern discipleship is the inversion of cause and effect. Many believers treat the Christian life as a project of self-improvement, as though the Scriptures were a behavioral science manual and virtue a form of personal achievement. But Jesus is not the reward for our progress; he is the root cause of all goodness. Our task is not to reengineer ourselves but to submit ourselves—believing, trusting, surrendering our will to his. The better life grows from the better Lord enthroned within. The same inversion appears in the way many speak of "purpose." We imagine Christ joining our journey, blessing our goals, strengthening our plans. But we are not the architects of his story; we are the servants within it. He directs the mission; we obey. When we reverse these truths, pride presents itself as devotion, and narcissism dresses as calling. Such inversion is more than immaturity—it becomes a foothold for darkness, allowing us to think we are doing God's work even while resisting his rule. Faithful resistance therefore begins within us, resisting not only the pressures of the age but the illusions of self, until our purpose is his and our strength is trust.

Faith is also the soil from which conscience grows. Knowledge of God gives the conscience its direction; assent to his Word gives it conviction; and trust in his Spirit gives it endurance. Without faith, conscience becomes mere instinct—noble, but blind. With faith, it becomes illuminated, judging rightly because it listens to the One who judges justly. Every act of faithful resistance is therefore an act of faith first and courage second. The believer resists not because he is strong, but because he trusts the strength of Another.

The pillars of this faith stand firm through every age. We believe in God—the Triune Creator, sovereign over all that is seen and unseen, perfect in grace and truth, whose mercy and righteousness form the foundation of existence. We believe in his eternal plan, revealed in Scripture, inspired and inerrant, fulfilled in Christ, offering eternal life to all who believe. We believe in Christ himself—God incarnate, crucified for sin, risen from death, reigning forever. In him, the debt of guilt is settled, the curse reversed, and the door to life opened. We believe in man—created in God's image, fallen in sin, redeemed by grace, destined for eternity. We believe in the Holy Spirit—who indwells and conforms believers to the likeness of Christ. We believe in the church—the living body of Christ, his spiritual house on earth. And we believe in the new Jerusalem—where redeemed souls and glorified bodies will dwell with God forever in perfect light.

Such faith does not remove struggle; it redeems it. It transforms fear into prayer, weakness into dependence, and endurance into witness. Every test of conscience becomes a test of faith—whether the believer will trust the unseen goodness of God above the seen power of men. Faith makes resistance possible because it makes obedience joyful. It anchors courage in eternity, freeing the soul from the tyranny of circumstance.

Faith is the first resistance and the last. It begins when the soul believes God rather than appearances, and it ends when the believer sees what he once only trusted. Stand therefore not in resolve, but in faith. Let knowledge of Christ shape your reason, assent to his word shape your conscience, and trust in his Spirit shape your life. For the just shall live by faith—and only those who live by faith can resist without hatred, obey without fear, and endure without despair.

Faithful Resistance

CALL TO FAITHFUL RESISTANCE— FAITH IN ACTION

Announce your faith in Christ—first to him, then to the world. Confess with your mouth that Jesus is Lord and believe in your heart that God raised him from the dead (Rom 10:9). Declare your allegiance publicly through baptism (Acts 2:38), and walk daily in active trust, joining the fellowship of believers who bear his name (Heb 10:24–25). Faith that hides itself is not faith at all, for Christ said, "Whoever acknowledges me before others, I will also acknowledge before my Father in heaven" (Matt 10:32). Let your profession become your practice—faith not as sentiment but as submission, not as doctrine alone but as life transformed.

To walk in faith is to walk in the opposite of the spirit of evil. Every faithful act is a reversal of the corruption that began in pride. Faith submits what evil exalts; it humbles the will, awakens the conscience, restores truth, and loves light more than approval. Where the world hardens, faith yields. Where the proud conceal, faith confesses. Where deception clouds, faith clarifies.

Submit your will to Christ. Pride resists surrender, but faith kneels first: "Not my will, but yours be done" (Luke 22:42). Every act of obedience disarms the tyranny of self and enthrones the Lord within. Keep your conscience alive before God. Evil denies sin; faith names it and repents. "If we confess our sins, he is faithful and just to forgive" (1 John 1:9). Let no self-deception survive the light of truth. The awakened conscience is the lamp of the Spirit within the soul (Prov 20:27).

Refuse projection and scapegoating. Evil blames others to escape judgment; faith accepts the cross and takes responsibility. "Each one should test their own actions" (Gal 6:4). The faithful see others not as enemies to accuse but as image bearers to redeem. Seek affirmation from God, not men. Evil demands admiration; faith seeks approval only from the Father. "Beware of practicing your righteousness before others to be seen by them" (Matt 6:1). The faithful do not wear masks of virtue—they live in the open air of grace.

The Faith of Faithful Resistance

Guard your mind against the spirit of unreality. Evil twists truth into confusion; faith renews the mind in the knowledge of Christ. "Take captive every thought to make it obedient to Christ" (2 Cor 10:5). Let reason be ruled by revelation, for Satan is the father of lies and the author of illusion.

Therefore, let faith become your resistance: submit rather than exalt, confess rather than conceal, take responsibility rather than accuse, seek truth rather than applause, live in reality rather than deception. For the faithful are not merely believers—they are witnesses, lights set against the dark. Announce your faith, live your confession, and let the world see the difference between coercion and conviction, between illusion and truth, between self and Christ.

> 1 Tim 6:12—"Fight the good fight of the faith. Take hold of the eternal life to which you were called."

REFLECTION

Faithful resistance begins where faith becomes visible. The battle for the conscience is not won by willpower but by worship—by hearts surrendered to the truth they profess. Evil thrives in the life not submitted to Christ, but faith exposes and heals it. When believers live what they confess, the kingdom advances not by the sword of coercion or the slogans of pride, but by one obedient conscience at a time. To walk in this faith is to make the unseen rule of Christ visible in the world—to become, in every generation, the living proof that truth still reigns.

CHAPTER 17

Truth and Coercion

John 8:32—"Then you will know the truth,
and the truth will set you free."

"Coercion is the counterfeit of conviction."
—*Faithful Resistance*, ch. 17

Human history is the story of truth under pressure. From Eden to empire, from the Sanhedrin to the modern state, one conflict endures: truth freely received versus "truth" forcefully imposed. The first is God's voice; the second is the voice of every usurper. Coercion is the counterfeit of conviction. It imitates obedience without touching the heart. It can compel words and ceremonies but never faith. Faith lives only where truth is free. When "truth" is enforced, it ceases to bear witness to God and begins to serve tyranny.

THE NATURE OF COERCION

Systems that distrust conscience will enslave it. Coercion rarely arrives with chains; it arrives with comforts—unity at the price of personhood, safety at the cost of sincerity, peace through silenced dissent. It promises progress without principle, virtue without repentance, belonging without belief. It thrives in church and court alike. Its fruit exposes it: uniformity without purity, obedience without love, crowds without conviction. Coercion builds empires, not kingdoms—and every empire falls. The conscience awakened by the Spirit will not sleep forever. Truth, once whispered, echoes. No decree or prison can contain its sound.

THE SPIRIT OF VIOLENCE AGAINST TRUTH

> John 15:18—"If the world hates you, keep in mind that it hated Me first."

When truth can no longer be refuted, it is attacked. Those who have replaced revelation with will must defend illusion with force. The world that has forgotten God's authority fears those who still live under it. Thus, when believers speak moral truth, a fallen culture interprets it as domination—because domination is the only kind of authority it still understands.

This is the great projection of the age. Those who worship power accuse the faithful of seeking it. Those who silence others cry "intolerance." Those who demand control call conviction "fascism." It is not misunderstanding but inversion—the guilty conscience defending its rebellion by accusing obedience of tyranny. The world projects its own violence onto those who still believe in moral order, imagining that what it would enforce with weapons, the church must also desire to enforce with words.

This is not confusion; it is spiritual hostility—the mind of the flesh warring against the Spirit of truth. When the conscience is silenced, conviction becomes the enemy. The age that celebrates "living your own truth" must persecute those who proclaim that truth is not owned but owed—to God.

Violence against truth takes many forms. Sometimes it shouts in anger or strikes in hatred; more often it shames, censors, and isolates. Yet whether by gun or gavel, social ridicule or public policy, the aim is the same: to drive conscience from the public square. The spirit that crucified Christ still hunts his witnesses, now dressed in the robes of tolerance.

The faithful must therefore see clearly what the world denies—that coercion always follows the rejection of revelation. When men cannot bear correction, they will persecute conviction. The believer must be prepared, not for argument alone, but for endurance.

This spirit has already shown its face in our generation—when those who merely speak truth are branded as threats, when courage is answered with mobs or bullets, when pulpits grow timid in the shadow of accusation. Yet truth has always walked this road. From prophets stoned to apostles imprisoned, from reformers burned to modern voices silenced, the lineage of faithful resistance stands unbroken.

The church must discern this hour. What the timid call "politics," heaven recognizes as the testing of truth. To hide behind neutrality is to abandon stewardship. The watchmen who refuse to warn will answer for the silence that follows.

Here the battle of every age is revealed. When illusion can no longer persuade, it must persecute. Yet every blow against truth only proves its endurance. The fire that consumes straw refines gold. Every attempt to silence conscience becomes its amplifier, for truth does not retreat—it rises through suffering.

The test of this generation is not whether truth will survive, but whether the faithful will still recognize it when it costs them comfort. The hour of violence against truth is also the hour of purification for the church, when false courage falls silent and real conviction learns to sing in chains.

THE NATURE OF TRUTH

Truth is not fragile. It does not need force to stand; it stands because it is real—because it reflects God himself. Lies require coercion; truth requires freedom. Christ refused compulsion. He invited, warned, and loved; he never manipulated. His kingdom grows by consent—hearts transformed, not conquered. "Everyone on the side of truth listens to me" (John 18:37). Pilate's "What is truth?"

was not inquiry but evasion—the reflex of rulers who sense they must bow if they admit it. Denial of truth is the tyrant's first law.

THE TYRANNY OF THE RELIGIOUS MIND

The subtlest coercion is religious—truth as creed without compassion, faith as fear of disapproval. A church that forgets grace mirrors the empires it once defied: policing souls, multiplying rules, mistaking control for holiness. The instinct that forged a golden calf can also gild a cathedral. God is not served by compulsion. Only the Spirit governs the soul without violating it. Prophets thundered to call, not to crush; apostles preached to deliver, not to dominate. Wherever faith has flourished, it has done so under freedom—the freedom to believe, to repent, even to err and be corrected by grace. The Spirit will not break a bruised reed; he strengthens it by truth.

TRUTH AND THE FREEDOM OF CONSCIENCE

Freedom of conscience is not a mere political doctrine; it is divine design—the atmosphere in which truth breathes. Conscience cannot operate under duress; fear drowns God's inward voice. Every true reformation, revival, and republic sought liberty for obedience—the liberty to hear and follow God without interference. This is the moral oxygen of civilization. Where it is absent, faith suffocates and tyranny thrives. The church must guard this freedom, even when mocked for it. To yield to coercion is to deny the Lord who conquers by truth, not force.

THE PATTERN OF CHRIST

The cross is the final refutation of coercion. Power nailed Truth to a tree to silence him; that death became power's defeat. Christ overthrew tyranny by enduring it. His refusal to coerce—even his captors—revealed love's sovereignty. The kingdom's paradox holds: it wins by losing, conquers by surrender, reigns by serving. "My kingdom is not of this world" means it is not vulnerable to the world.

THE CONSCIENCE OF NATIONS

Individuals who live by truth make nations possible; individuals who live by coercion make nations decay. Conscience is the smallest and strongest government. Civil order rests on moral order; moral order rests on truth freely embraced. Tyrants demand obedience without understanding; God seeks obedience born of love. Societies rise or fall by how they treat truth—gift or threat. Freedom without truth collapses into chaos; truth without freedom hardens into despotism. Only together do they yield righteousness.

THE PERIL OF APOSTASY

There is a surrender darker than fear before tyrants—the surrender of truth itself. Apostasy is not ignorance but betrayal: agreement with deception after knowing the light. It begins in silence, grows by compromise, ends in blindness. The conscience that once trembled learns to prefer shadow. The final deception will come dressed as compassion—mercy without repentance, unity without truth. It will persuade more than persecute, offering peace in exchange for purity. Many will bow, not from hatred of God but from weariness of standing alone. Each accommodation rehearses denial; each denial erases conviction. To be "blotted out" is not the act of an irrational Judge but the end of a will that chose darkness. What departs from truth departs from life. The church's greatest danger is not the sword but the smile of compromise. Yet grace does not retreat. The Judge still calls. Though many grow cold, Christ's mercy burns brighter. The story of conscience ends not in apostasy but in the Lamb's faithfulness.

The final rebellion will appear as moral authority divorced from God—the beast ruling without the Lamb, and the false prophet speaking without the Spirit. It will promise justice without repentance, belonging without belief, and unity without truth. What God gave as revelation will be recast as control. The last deception will not abolish worship—it will redirect it.

THE TRIUMPH OF GRACE

Truth cannot be coerced because love cannot be forced. Christ reigns not by statute or sword but by renewed hearts. Every redeemed conscience is a kingdom within; every faithful act is a declaration of independence from sin. The victory of truth is present as well as future—wherever light unmasks lies and mercy conquers fear. The world still wields censorship, corruption, and violence, but its defeat is already written: "The kingdom of the world has become the kingdom of our Lord and of his Christ" (Rev 11:15).

THE FINAL UNION

Scripture foresees a last alliance of throne and altar—power and piety joined against God. The beast and the false prophet will counterfeit church and state: a piety without holiness and a state without conscience. It will preach order without obedience, virtue without repentance, worship without the cross. Even then, the faithful will not be without light. The Spirit who sustained Daniel and John will sustain the church. Her victory will be clarity—the witness of truth that outlasts the thrones that despise it.

CALL TO FAITHFUL RESISTANCE—STAND IN THE DAY OF TESTING

The age of counterfeit peace is upon us. It preaches mercy without repentance and unity without truth. It praises tolerance but punishes holiness. It calls conviction cruelty and faithfulness extremism. Yet truth, once spoken, cannot be silenced.

When courage is slandered as violence, stand your post. When shepherds call danger "politics," remember that the wolves do not share their restraint. The line between church and world is being tested again—not by policy but by persecution disguised as civility.

Refuse to fear what the world threatens. Stand firm where others hedge. The task of the watchman is not comfort but clarity; his reward is not safety but sight. Preach while it costs something. Lead where it risks reputation. Let gentleness remain your manner, but conviction your core.

The church does not preserve herself by silence but by testimony. Truth still conquers by persuasion, not force; by endurance, not violence. The cross remains the answer to every tyranny of the soul.

Guard the lamp of conscience. Speak light where the world demands shadow. The Lamb still reigns, and his truth does not seek permission to shine. Stand until the kingdoms of this world become the kingdom of our Lord and of his Christ.

> 2 Cor 3:17—"Now the Lord is the Spirit, and where the Spirit of the Lord is, there is freedom."

Resist control that silences conscience. Refuse "truth" enforced by fear. Stand free of false peace. Let courage rise in love, and truth burn brighter than hatred.

What follows in the appendices is not an interruption but an extension. Each topic deepens the foundation laid in these chapters—truths about conscience, authority, and the moral order that require closer attention. They are offered not as separate essays but as additional beams supporting the house.

EPILOGUE

The Freedom of the Faithful

Faithful Resistance ends not in revolt but in renewal. It is the continual refusal to surrender conscience to control. The believer who abides in truth stands taller than kings and freer than rebels. His allegiance is eternal; his peace, unassailable.

The story that began on the seat of Moses finds its completion on the throne of the Lamb. Law has become life; command has become communion. In him, the Prophet who revealed truth, the Priest who redeemed sinners, and the King who reigns in righteousness are one. The moral, civil, and ceremonial orders—once divided by sin—are reconciled in Christ and written upon the hearts of his people through the Holy Spirit.

And the people of conscience—those who feared God more than Pharaoh, who loved truth more than safety, who endured rather than complied—will reign with him, not as masters, but as servants of the Light. For truth, once set free, never bows again.

POSTLUDE

The Story of Conscience

Rom 13:12—"The night is nearly over; the day is almost here. So let us put aside the deeds of darkness and put on the armor of light."

The story of *Faithful Resistance* is the story of conscience—the divine thread that runs through creation, law, history, and redemption. It begins not with man's striving but with God's speaking. At Sinai, that voice thundered through cloud and fire, engraving holiness upon stone. At Calvary, it whispered through blood and mercy, engraving the same holiness upon the human heart.

The seat of Moses, once the symbol of divine judgment, has become through Christ the seat of divine indwelling. What was external has become internal. What was enforced by law is now embraced by love. Humanity, once governed by tablets and kings, is now invited into the inner kingdom where God rules through conscience—the meeting place of truth and freedom.

FROM LAW TO LIFE

Through the centuries, men have tried to govern without God and worship without conscience. Both pursuits end in tyranny. The law of God is not a chain but a structure, not a burden but a boundary. It is the architecture of moral freedom—the frame in which love can flourish without fear.

POSTLUDE

The tragedy of history has been the confusion of this divine order. Kings sought to rule in God's name, priests sought to command the conscience, and nations built empires of coercion upon the ruins of faith. Yet in every age, God raised voices—prophets, apostles, reformers, and witnesses—to recall his people to the law written within.

This is the rhythm of redemptive history: revelation, corruption, resistance, and renewal. The law is revealed, man distorts it, conscience resists, and grace restores. Through it all, conscience remains the instrument of covenant—the means by which heaven tutors the heart. And through every cycle, the throne of heaven is reflected more clearly in the heart of the redeemed.

THE ENDURING LAW OF RESISTANCE

Faithful resistance is not rebellion; it is reverence in motion. It is the refusal to bow to what contradicts truth and the courage to obey God when obedience costs dearly. The midwives of Egypt, the prophets of Israel, the martyrs of Rome, the Reformers of Europe, and the confessors of modern times all walked this same narrow road between submission and defiance.

Their witness declares one enduring truth: coercion cannot conquer conviction. The conscience governed by Christ is untouchable. It may be imprisoned, exiled, or killed—but it cannot be conquered. For it is ruled by a higher law, one that does not change with kings or councils.

The measure of a civilization is not its wealth or power, but the moral integrity of its people—the degree to which conscience remains free under God. When conscience is silenced, tyranny begins. When conscience awakens, history turns.

The Story of Conscience

THE KINGDOM WITHIN AND THE KINGDOM TO COME

All authority, civil and sacred, will one day bow before the King whose scepter is righteousness. The kingdoms of this world will pass away, but the kingdom of conscience—the reign of truth within the heart—endures forever.

This kingdom is not metaphor but reality already unfolding. Each act of faithful conscience is a foretaste of that final order when justice and mercy meet. The believer who walks in this kingdom becomes both citizen and ambassador—governed by heaven yet dwelling on earth. He resists not from pride but from purity; not to destroy authority but to redeem it.

His life becomes living proof that divine government can dwell in human form. This is the mystery of faith: the God who once wrote his law on stone now writes his likeness on souls. The throne of heaven and the conscience of man are not rivals but reflections—one infinite, one intimate, both eternal henceforth.

THE FINAL HARVEST

The harvest principle that guided this work reaches its fulfillment here. The field of history, sown with both wheat and counterfeit seed, is not abandoned but tended. Every act of faithful resistance, every defense of truth, every quiet obedience adds to that harvest—not of temporal triumph, but of eternal souls gathered into light.

God's harvest is not of nations but of hearts; not of monuments, but of lives transformed by Truth. When the final gathering comes, the faithful of every age will know one another by the same flame—the law of God shining through the conscience redeemed by grace.

POSTLUDE
THE SEAT RESTORED

So the story ends where it began—not in power, but in Presence. The seat of Moses has become the seat of Christ; the throne of judgment has become the mercy seat. Law and love, authority and conscience, resistance and redemption have found their unity in him.

The believer now stands as steward of this mystery—a witness to truth amid coercion, a vessel of grace amid pride. His resistance is faithful because his allegiance is eternal. He obeys not to escape wrath but to reflect glory. And in that obedience, the world sees again what it was meant to be: a creation ordered by conscience, governed by truth, and illuminated by the everlasting light of God.

"The night is nearly over; the day is almost here." Let every soul, therefore, put on the armor of light—and stand.

THE CONTINUING WITNESS OF CONSCIENCE

The story of *Faithful Resistance* does not end with history—it continues in reflection. What follows are meditations that extend the work of the book beyond the visible struggle into the hidden formation of the soul. Each appendix stands as a separate seat of witness: the boundary between church and state, the schooling of conscience, the fire of prophecy, the vigilance of the watchman, the perception of divine order, and the challenge of conscience in an age of machines. Together they form the living echo of the seat of Moses—proof that the law written on the heart still speaks in every realm where truth must stand against coercion.

APPENDIX I

Separation of Church and State

Matt 22:21—"Render to Caesar what is Caesar's, and to God what is God's."

THE BOUNDARY CHRIST DREW

The boundary Christ drew with a single sentence remains one of history's most misunderstood lines. When he spoke those words, he was not dividing the world into sacred and secular halves; he was restoring order to both. "Render to Caesar" affirmed the legitimacy of civil rule; "and to God" reinthroned the conscience as its higher court. In that balance, the kingdoms of this world were called to accountability, and the kingdom of heaven was revealed as their moral measure.

THE ORIGIN OF THE BOUNDARY

In Israel, the law itself had contained both altar and judgment seat. The priest and the magistrate served under one covenant, each reflecting a different facet of divine authority. When that unity was corrupted—when kings assumed priestly power or priests sought political favor—the harmony of heaven fractured upon the earth. The prophets cried against this confusion, warning that God's throne cannot be shared with human ambition.

Appendix I

Christ's words in the temple courts restored what the prophets foresaw. Standing before those who sought to trap him between loyalty and treason, he spoke the principle that would govern conscience for all ages: no earthly power may claim what belongs to God alone. Authority over life and property may be delegated to Caesar, but authority over truth and worship belongs eternally to the Lord.

Yet those words were not only a boundary for kingdoms; they were a mirror for souls. The Pharisees and the Herodians had not come to debate taxation but to test allegiance. Their question was crafted to force a false choice—either bless Roman oppression or spark open revolt. But Christ exposed the lie beneath the dilemma. He divided the jurisdictions without dividing the allegiance of the soul. He upheld Caesar's office while stripping Caesar of any divine claim.

This is why Matthew records that they "were amazed and left him" (Matt 22:22). The force of his answer shattered their categories. Their amazement was the confession they dared not speak: Christ had redrawn the boundary they had blurred, revealing their misuse of both religion and power.

His reply turned their trap into a question that still echoes in every heart: What do you render, and to whom? The coin bears Caesar's image, but the soul bears God's. To render to God what is God's is to return the image to its Maker—to give him not silver, but self. Thus the issue is never merely political; it is personal. Every generation must answer anew: Where does our allegiance lie—with God, or with the world?

THE CORRUPTION OF THE BOUNDARY

History's tragedies began when this boundary blurred. When emperors baptized their armies, when bishops crowned kings, when faith became the language of empire, the conscience lost its liberty. The union of altar and throne produced order without righteousness and power without repentance. The same sword that once defended the innocent was soon raised against dissent. The church that should have judged kings became their chaplain; the state that should have feared God began to use his name as sanction.

Yet even amid the confusion, the pattern of restoration continued. Reformers rose to remind rulers that grace cannot be legislated, and prophets reminded prelates that power cannot sanctify itself. From the catacombs of Rome to the fields of Wittenberg, conscience rediscovered its voice. The Reformation did not abolish authority—it purified it, returning law to its civil sphere and faith to its spiritual one.

When the gospel reentered history as freedom of conscience, it prepared the soil for liberty of law. The same truth that freed the church from Rome would, in time, free the state from coercion.

THE CORRUPTION OF THE AMENDMENT

The simplest way to understand the intent of the First Amendment regarding religious liberty is to see how it was meant to operate: faith, or the lack thereof, cannot be discriminated against. The government may neither establish a religion nor persecute those who practice one. The amendment was not written to protect the state from faith, but to protect faith from the state.

Yet in our time, the language of liberty has been quietly inverted. The phrase "separation of church and state," once a fence to keep tyranny from entering the sanctuary, has been rebuilt as a wall to keep truth from entering the public square. The result is a legal fiction that grants unbelief the privileges of belief and treats conscience as a private eccentricity rather than a public trust.

Such reasoning does not create neutrality; it enthrones a rival faith. When the state excludes God from law and policy, it does not become secular—it becomes its own religion, offering the worship of power in place of the worship of holiness. This is the hidden liturgy of an antichrist order: a government that baptizes unbelief and enthrones the will of man beneath a halo of progress.

The watchman must therefore warn: the First Amendment is being turned against the very liberty it was written to preserve. To command believers to keep their faith within their churches is to declare the public realm the property of darkness. The covenant vision of the founders—law under God, conscience free before him—is being replaced by a counterfeit freedom in which the only forbidden creed is obedience to Christ.

True religious liberty does not mean the absence of faith in public life; it means that no earthly power may compel the conscience against the law of God. To defend that liberty is not rebellion; it is faithfulness.

THE CONSCIENCE AND THE KINGDOM

For the believer, this boundary is not merely civic but spiritual. The faithful serve within Caesar's world but answer to Christ's throne. To obey just laws is duty; to sanctify conscience is devotion. The disciple renders unto Caesar taxes and service, but renders unto God truth and loyalty. The former may command the hand, but only the latter commands the heart.

Thus the true separation is not between God and government, but between coercion and conviction. The kingdom of God is not built by ballots or decrees but by hearts transformed through grace. When the church keeps her altar pure, she becomes once again the conscience of nations. When the state honors that conscience, it becomes an instrument of peace rather than oppression.

CLOSING REFLECTION

The boundary Christ drew remains the world's last safeguard of liberty. It reminds kings that their power is borrowed, and priests that their calling is bound to humility. It declares that truth needs no throne, for its authority flows from the One who reigns forever.

So long as men remember this word—"Render to Caesar what is Caesar's, and to God what is God's"—the balance of heaven will still order the affairs of earth. And when that balance is forgotten, the faithful must remember it anew, for the seat of Moses stands again in every conscience awakened by the Spirit of the living God.

Separation of Church and State
CALL TO FAITHFUL RESISTANCE—CONSCIENCE UNCHAINED

The line Christ drew still divides the living from the loyal. Caesar may tax your labor, but he may not claim your soul. When rulers demand silence about righteousness, the faithful must answer as the apostles did: *"We must obey God rather than men."*

The public square is no longer neutral ground; it has become a battlefield of ideas and idols. Yet the light does not retreat from darkness—it enters it. Go where truth is mocked, where faith is forbidden, where conscience is ridiculed, and speak without fear. You are not an intruder there; you are an ambassador of a greater kingdom.

The state may govern conduct, but it cannot govern conscience. Speak truth where policy forbids it. Worship where law would limit it. Refuse the bargain of comfort for compromise. The liberty of nations endures only where the fear of God outlives the fear of men.

Therefore stand in the public square as one who bears a higher allegiance. Render to Caesar duty, but render to Christ dominion. Let your words be gracious but unbending, your courage visible, your faith public yet pure. For tyranny begins when conscience bows, and renewal begins when it speaks.

> Matt 22:21—"Render to Caesar what is Caesar's, and to God what is God's."

Give the state your duty, not your devotion. Keep worship unowned by politics. Resist laws that demand moral silence. Speak God's truth where others forbid it. Let conscience remain indivisible.

APPENDIX II

The Prophetic Voice

Jer 1:10—"See, I appoint you this day over nations and kingdoms to uproot and tear down, to destroy and to overthrow, to build and to plant."

The prophetic voice is the conscience of creation—

the fire of truth spoken in love,

tearing down the idols of pride

and planting the seeds of holiness anew.

Jer 20:9—"His word is in my heart like a fire, a fire shut up in my bones; I am weary of holding it in; indeed, I cannot."

THE FIRE WITHIN

Every generation inherits both the call and the temptation—to speak for God, yet in its own image. The true prophet is born not of outrage but of obedience. His power is purity of motive; his authority is surrender of will. The moment the prophetic word becomes a weapon of pride, it ceases to be divine. The church must therefore guard its fire from the pollution of fury.

To speak prophetically is to feel the word like flame and still let it burn through mercy. Truth without tenderness hardens; compassion without conviction dissolves. The prophetic voice lives between the two—a sword tempered by tears.

TRUTH IN A MODERN WILDERNESS

Our own age, loud with opinion and weary of wisdom, needs the prophet more than the pundit. The world prizes visibility; God prizes vision. The true prophetic spirit will not trade moral clarity for cultural approval nor confuse social noise with spiritual authority. Its message is not, "Look at us," but, "Return to him."

Modern prophecy must therefore recover reverence. It must learn again that rebuke without holiness is performance, and prediction without repentance is vanity. The aim of the prophet is not to win an argument but to awaken a people—to call the soul of a generation back to the law written on the heart.

GUARDING THE TONE OF HEAVEN

The danger of our time is not absence of speech but the loss of sacred speech. Words once reserved for prayer have become slogans; indignation masquerades as insight. Yet the Spirit does not anoint resentment. The voice of God is firm but never cruel, corrective yet always redemptive.

Every believer who speaks for truth must first kneel before it. The tongue that has not trembled in God's presence will tremble before men. The prophet's authority is measured not by volume but by virtue—by the holiness that silences hypocrisy. A sentence whispered in purity carries more weight in heaven than a thousand shouted in pride.

The Prophetic Voice

THE PROPHETIC CALL OF THE CHURCH

The church herself is the corporate prophet to the nations. Her task is not to echo the spirit of the age but to expose it by contrast. She must comfort the afflicted without flattering the comfortable; she must stand near the sinner while refusing his sin. When the church speaks truth in love, she does not conquer culture; she converts it.

To bear the prophetic mantle today is to live transparently—to be what one proclaims. The world believes integrity long before it believes theology. The holiness of the messenger is the credibility of the message.

Our age multiplies speech but not repentance. Many perform righteousness in the glare of public platforms yet refuse holiness in private rooms. The appearance of virtue has become a substitute for its practice. But the Spirit does not anoint performance. The prophet must therefore live unseen faith before proclaiming seen truth, for moral theater cannot awaken a sleeping world. Only authenticity kindled in secret sustains authority in public.

THE FALSE PROPHETS OF KNOWLEDGE

Not all prophecy speaks in thunder. Some deceive by reason. Through the centuries, a quieter temptation has visited the church—the worship of knowledge divorced from holiness. Ancient Gnosticism claimed that salvation came through secret wisdom; modern ideologies preach the same with new vocabularies. Whether in the philosopher king who rules by intellect, the Marxist who promises justice through revolution, or the modern moralist who claims authority by social, scientific, or cultural enlightenment rather than repentance and renewal—each repeats the serpent's whisper: "You will be like God." Thus the oldest heresy survives beneath new vocabularies—the worship of intellect as salvation.

In the Platonic hierarchy of knowledge, *episteme* stood above opinion as the possession of ultimate truth—the philosopher's ascent from shadow to Form. Yet when a man declares, *"Ego eimi he tou alethous episteme"* ("I am the science of the true"), he does not merely claim understanding; he assumes the throne of Truth itself. Here the intellect ceases to serve revelation and begins to rival it. What was meant to be the lamp of reason becomes the idol of it. The prophets bowed before the Word; the philosophers bowed before the mind. In this inversion lies the peril of every age—when knowledge forgets its Source and the creature speaks as though he were the Creator.

The prophetic conscience answers otherwise: "Be holy, for I am holy." Revelation, not speculation, redeems the world. Truth is not ascended to but descended upon. The cross remains the end of every false enlightenment, for there the wisdom of man dies and the wisdom of God begins. Faithful resistance stands in that light—humble, embodied, and obedient—confessing that the only true knowledge is to know him who is Truth.

This ancient deceit, once clothed in theology, now reappears in the machinery of modern intellect. What the church once discerned as heresy it must now name as ideology. The false prophets of knowledge have traded pulpits for platforms, but the spirit is unchanged—the worship of intellect without holiness. That same spirit now governs through algorithm and ambition, promising progress while exalting the self against the sovereignty of God.

A subtler deception follows—the worship of feeling as truth. Modern compassion, unanchored from holiness, becomes sentimentality that blesses what God forbids and excuses what conscience condemns. The prophet must love deeply but never at the expense of reality. Mercy severed from righteousness ceases to heal; it merely hides the wound. True compassion calls sin by name so that grace may restore what guilt has broken.

THE VOICE THAT ENDURES

The prophetic word endures because it is not anchored in circumstance but in character. It remains when empires fall and ideologies decay. Every era that has silenced its prophets has awakened to judgment; every era that has heard them has found renewal. The church must therefore cherish the voices that discomfort her, for they are the instruments of her cleansing.

The true prophet does not divide God's people but calls them to repentance. His cry is the same in every century: "Return to the Lord." Whether spoken from a pulpit, a prison, or a quiet conscience, that call is the heartbeat of heaven within the noise of earth.

Yet the false light does not rest. What once hid in the councils of philosophy now breathes through circuits and screens. The same spirit that tempted man to worship his own mind has found new form in the machinery of intellect—code without conscience, power without prayer. The prophets of old warned of idols made by human hands; ours are made by human minds. And still the call endures: to discern the living Spirit from the synthetic one, and to bow only to the Word that became flesh.

CLOSING REFLECTION

To speak for God is to die to vanity. The prophetic voice is not a platform but a burden—the privilege of carrying light through storm. Let every believer who feels that fire guard its flame with humility, lest it scorch rather than sanctify. For the world is not changed by anger, but by holiness aflame with truth. And when that truth is spoken in love, the fire of the prophet becomes the light of the church.

CALL TO FAITHFUL RESISTANCE—THE FIRE THAT CANNOT BE IMITATED

The spirit of antichrist still speaks in the voice of enlightenment. It does not deny light; it defines it. It promises truth without holiness and progress without repentance. It flatters intellect while mocking obedience. Yet every brilliance not born of the Spirit ends in blindness.

Therefore let the faithful stand where deception shines brightest. Speak when truth is costly. Confront the wisdom that exalts itself against God. Test every vision by the cross and every revelation by repentance. Do not fear being called foolish by those who worship knowledge, for the wisdom of God still confounds the wise.

Guard your heart from pride and your tongue from wrath, but let your silence never join the lie. The world needs prophets more than pundits, witnesses more than experts. Let your words burn with holiness, not hatred. For only fire from heaven exposes the counterfeit light of hell.

> Jer 20:9—"His word is in my heart like a fire, a fire shut up in my bones; I am weary of holding it in; indeed, I cannot."

Speak when truth burns within you. Refuse the comfort of silence. Let compassion steady your rebuke. Honor God more than approval. Prophesy in holiness, not anger.

APPENDIX III

The Watchman's Seat

Ezek 33:3—"When he sees the sword coming on the land and blows the trumpet to warn the people."

The watchman stands between warning and mercy—
a sentinel of conscience on the wall of time,
whose vigilance becomes intercession
and whose cry prepares the way of the Lord.

Ezek 33:7—"Son of man, I have made you a watchman for the people of Israel; so hear the word I speak and give them warning from Me."

THE CALL TO VIGILANCE

The calling of the watchman is as ancient as the wall. From the ramparts of Jerusalem to the pulpits of the church, and from the trembling edges of history to the quiet corners of conscience, God has appointed voices to see before others see and to speak before others dare. The watchman does not choose his post; he inherits it. His burden is vigilance, his reward is obedience, and his failure is silence.

Appendix III

In every generation, God raises those who can discern the hour. The watchman sees what comfort cannot. He looks not at the surface of events but at the moral currents beneath them—the slow corrosion of conscience, the subtle exalting of pride, the quiet normalization of sin. His eyes are trained by prayer, his ears tuned to the Spirit. While others rest, he listens for the tremor that precedes collapse.

To watch is to love. The vigilant heart does not warn from superiority but from compassion. The sentry who cries out at night is not condemning the city; he is preserving it. The true watchman would rather be mocked than mute, for he knows that silence is complicity.

THE SEAT OF ACCOUNTABILITY

The watchman's seat is not a throne but a stewardship. It stands wherever conscience stands upright—on a wall, in a pulpit, in the quiet of a prayer closet. To sit upon it is to bear the weight of moral sight. The one who sees and fails to speak answers for the blood he might have spared (Ezek 33:8). Yet even this warning is mercy, for God entrusts his watchmen not with omniscience but with obedience.

Every believer shares this calling. Royalty under Christ the King must also be sentinels under his command. The parent who guards the soul of a child, the pastor who guards the purity of a flock, the citizen who guards the conscience of a nation—all keep watch upon some portion of the wall. The seat belongs not to the powerful but to the faithful.

THE DISCIPLINE OF DISCERNMENT

The modern world rewards noise but neglects discernment. The true watchman must therefore learn to see without panic and to speak without pride. He must test every alarm against the word of God, lest zeal become error. Discernment is not suspicion; it is clarity born of holiness. In an age of endless data, the rarest sight is still the single eye—the heart undistracted by noise. The pure in heart see God because their vision is undivided. So too the watchman sees truth because his allegiance is singular.

He guards his tone as well as his message. Warning without hope wounds the weary; hope without warning flatters the deceived. The faithful watchman joins both: judgment seasoned with mercy, urgency restrained by peace.

THE WATCHMAN AND THE CHURCH

The church herself is the wall upon which the watchmen stand. When she forgets her post, nations stumble in darkness. Her task is not to predict history but to interpret it—to read the signs of the times through the lens of eternal truth. The prophet warns; the priest intercedes; the watchman does both. He cries from the wall and then falls to his knees, pleading that judgment might turn to mercy.

This is the posture of mature authority: eyes lifted, knees bent, heart pure. The church that watches in this way becomes the conscience of her age, steady amid storms, fearless amid fury.

CLOSING REFLECTION

To sit in the watchman's seat is to feel the weight of both warning and wonder. The view is broad, but the heart must stay humble. The watchman does not own the city he guards; he serves the King who built it. Let the faithful, then, keep watch—not in anxiety but in anticipation. For the dawn will come, and the One for whom we watch will appear. Until that day, vigilance remains worship, and the cry of every true watchman echoes still through time: "Prepare the way of the Lord."

APPENDIX III

CALL TO FAITHFUL RESISTANCE—THE COURAGE TO CRY OUT

The hour grows late, and many watchmen have left the wall. But the command remains: *Speak when others are silent; warn while mercy still waits.* The blood of a generation may rest on the voice that refused to sound the alarm.

Therefore take your post and keep it. See what others will not see; name what others fear to name. Let compassion move you, but let truth compel you. The warning of love is still love.

Cry out against the sins that sleep in comfort—the corruption that passes for policy, the idolatry that hides in entertainment, the cruelty that calls itself progress. The walls of nations crumble first in the silence of their watchmen.

Watch, pray, and speak until the dawn appears. For vigilance is not despair but devotion, and every cry of conscience is a candle against the dark. The trumpet still belongs to the faithful—lift it high, though the night resist you, for the King is near.

> Ezek 33:7—"Son of man, I have made you a watchman for the people of Israel; so hear the word I speak and give them warning from Me."

THE CONTINUING WITNESS OF CONSCIENCE

The watchmen of one age become the witnesses of the next. Their courage, recorded in history and sealed in blood, forms the living chain through which truth has endured. What follows is not mere remembrance but testimony—the lineage of holy conscience that carried light through centuries of shadow. Each name is a reminder that vigilance is never finished, and that the same Spirit who called them to stand now calls us to do likewise.

APPENDIX IV

Consciousness and Divine Order: The Soul and Spirit in God's Created Field

Ps 36:9—"For with You is the fountain of life;
in Your light we see light."

THE SEAT OF PERCEPTION

The final seat of *Faithful Resistance* stands not upon the earth but within the spirit—the inner Mount where perception becomes praise. Here the law fulfilled in Christ is transformed into sight, and the mind is restored to see as God intended. Consciousness is not creative power but redeemed awareness: the mirror through which truth is recognized and reflected. To see rightly is the final act of obedience.

Yet the clarity of sight is also a kind of warfare. For every revelation of truth exposes a countermovement of deception. The unseen realm is not imagination—it is the unseen order beneath the visible world, where spirits of light and darkness contend for the allegiance of human hearts. To discern rightly is to resist invisibly, for "solid food is for the mature, who by constant use have trained themselves to distinguish good from evil" (Heb 5:14).

Appendix IV

The gift of spiritual discernment, which Scripture names as a work of the Holy Spirit, is the conscience's participation in this hidden battle. Just as science reveals the structure of matter, revelation unveils the structure of meaning. The believer who perceives truth in the Spirit stands against falsehood not with argument but with presence—his very awareness becomes obedience. Thus consciousness is not merely perception; it is participation in God's ongoing resistance to evil.

THE SOUL AND THE SPIRIT

The soul feels; the spirit knows. The soul bears the story of the pilgrim—its affections, its fears, its longings. The spirit is the breath of God within man, the faculty of communion through which truth is received rather than discovered. The conscience is the meeting place of soul and spirit—the soul awakened by the Holy Spirit to recognize the truth he reveals. In this inner union, understanding becomes obedience and perception becomes worship, as the whole person is brought into harmony by the sanctifying work of the Spirit.

> Prov 20:27—"The spirit of man is the lamp of the LORD, searching all the inner depths of his heart."

When the Holy Spirit sanctifies the soul, feeling and knowing no longer contend but consent—the whole self becoming harmony in worship. Then the person himself becomes liturgy: mind illumined, will surrendered, heart aflame.

THE GIFT OF PERCEPTION

From the first moment God said, "Let there be light," creation became both visible and knowable. Every act of seeing since has been an echo of that Word.

> Rom 1:20—"For since the creation of the world God's invisible qualities—His eternal power and divine

nature—have been clearly seen, being understood from what has been made, so that people are without excuse."

Ps 19:1–4—"The heavens declare the glory of God. . . . Day after day they pour forth speech."

Consciousness is therefore a sacrament of light—the capacity to perceive order because order was first spoken into being. Faith does not invent reality; it awakens to it. By faith we understand that the universe was formed at God's command (Heb 11:3); and by that same faith we discern the moral structure that underlies the physical.

THE FABRIC OF CREATION

Science and Scripture gaze upon the same mystery from different vantage points. Science describes the behavior of matter; Scripture declares the motive of its Maker. Every law of nature is a sentence in the language of God. What physicists call the fabric of space and time is the ordered result of his Word—creation shaped to be knowable.

Creation itself is not conscious. Light does not perceive, and particles do not ponder. Yet the universe is structured so that the conscious mind can perceive the truth God has woven into it. Reality is not aware, but it is awareness-bearing—designed for discernment. This is the quiet fact that has unsettled secular science for generations: consciousness is not explained by the world; it explains the world. It is not produced by matter but awakened to meaning. The attempt to reduce awareness to neurons has only multiplied the mystery, for no physical process can give what it does not possess—self-knowledge, moral insight, or the ability to recognize truth. The first question is not how the brain produces consciousness, but how consciousness can know the brain.

The so-called "hard problem of consciousness" is not a puzzle to be solved but a boundary to be acknowledged. It marks the collision between the material world and the moral universe, between what science can measure and what only the soul can perceive. The

Appendix IV

observer effect in physics does not reveal awareness in matter but the precision of a world built for minds—a creation that yields its nature when examined because it was formed by the One who is Truth.

Physical light illuminates the eyes; spiritual light illuminates the heart, and the refusal to distinguish the two leads to confusion—not only in belief but in science itself. The confusion of the two has birthed ancient errors: materialism, which denies the Giver, and mysticism, which divinizes the gift. But creation remains what Scripture declares it to be—revelation in structure, awaiting recognition in the conscience. When the heart turns toward God, creation reveals the meaning he embedded within it.

THE COLLISION OF SCIENCE AND CONSCIENCE

Modern man has learned to split the atom but not his pride. He has measured light's speed but not its source. Yet science and conscience were never enemies; they are twin discoveries of the same truth—one explores God's creation, the other confesses his authorship. The collision between them is not warfare but awakening. It is the moment when the mind, in pursuit of knowledge, meets the mystery of holiness and must bow.

When knowledge is severed from gratitude, wisdom dies. The laboratory becomes a temple to pride, and the screen a mirror of self-worship. Data multiplies while discernment decays. The mind that refuses to glorify God will eventually lose the capacity to know him, mistaking complexity for creation and information for illumination.

> Prov 1:7—"The fear of the LORD is the beginning of knowledge."

For every law of physics that governs the visible world, there is a law of love that governs the soul. To study creation without worship is to map a kingdom and ignore its King. But to study it in reverence is to find that the same order that holds the stars in their courses holds the heart in peace.

THE RESTORED VISION

The cross did more than redeem the will; it restored the sight. In Christ, the mind is made whole, and creation is seen again as it was in Eden—a sanctuary of truth. To walk in the Spirit is to perceive the world not as matter to be mastered but as meaning to be revealed. The scientist at his lens, the poet at his page, and the saint at his knees are all participating in the same act—beholding the glory of God in the works of his hands.

THE COUNTERFEIT LIGHT

Yet not all illumination is holy. The spirit of deception clothes itself in brilliance, offering enlightenment without repentance and unity without God. From Eden's promise of secret knowledge to the modern creed of self-created truth, the same lie endures: that man may define the light for himself.

> 2 Cor 11:14—"Satan himself masquerades as an angel of light."

But true perception begins in surrender, not self-assertion. The conscience, illumined by grace, sees through false glory to divine reality. For every counterfeit illumination, the Spirit reveals the flame of holiness that cannot be imitated. To see truly is to discern the difference between wisdom that exalts man and revelation that glorifies God.

The new idols wear the vocabulary of progress—energy, vibration, collective awareness—but beneath the radiance is the same rebellion: man seeking to be as God. Enlightenment without repentance is still darkness, and unity without holiness is still separation.

The rebellion now takes another form—the denial of creation itself. In the name of freedom, men and women attempt to rewrite

Appendix IV

the image they were given, treating the body as canvas rather than covenant. Yet to remake the self is to reject the Giver; to claim authorship of being is to erase the grace of design. The spirit of unreality promises liberation but delivers estrangement, for no soul can find peace while it wars against its own created order.

CLOSING REFLECTION

When the soul perceives the order of creation, it is not mastering the world but worshiping its Maker. In that moment, the boundary between science and conscience becomes the threshold of praise. The same light that governs the atom governs the heart, and the same Word that upholds the universe illumines the believer's mind.

Thus the Seat of Perception completes the journey of *Faithful Resistance*—from law to love, from command to communion, from obedience to sight.

CALL TO FAITHFUL RESISTANCE—THE SIGHT OF CONSCIENCE

The light of creation leaves humanity without excuse. To look upon the world and deny its Author is not reason—it is rebellion. The materialist worships mechanism and calls it truth; the mystic worships awareness and calls it god. Both enthrone the creature and exile the Creator.

Faithful resistance begins where false light ends: in repentance. The conscience must bow before revelation, not imagination. Reality is not self-created but spoken; truth is not collective but personal—the Word through whom all things were made.

Therefore guard your sight. Let the world's brilliance not blind you to its Source. Resist the creed of the self-made universe and the gospel of impersonal unity. Stand fast in the light that judges as it illumines. For every denial of the Creator is a descent into darkness, but every act of holy perception is a victory of truth over illusion.

Contentiousness and Divine Order

Ps 36:9—"For with You is the fountain of life; in Your light we see light."

Keep perception anchored in holiness. Resist enlightenment that excludes God. Discern between brilliance and truth. Let your awareness become worship. See through light to its Source.

FROM DIVINE ORDER TO ARTIFICIAL IMITATION

As the conscience awakens to divine order within, it must also discern its counterfeit in the world without. The age now dawning seeks to imitate creation through machinery of its own making—minds without mercy, reason without reverence, power without prayer.

Yet no mechanism can bear the image of God, for conscience cannot be programmed; it must be received. Thus the final discernment of our time is between image and imitation—between the living breath of God and the lifeless circuitry of control.

The next reflection turns from the soul illumined by Spirit to the machine devoid of it—from the created field of light to the cold lattice of self-made order.

APPENDIX V

The Machine Without Conscience

Ps 115:4-8—"Their idols are silver and gold, made by human hands. They have mouths, but cannot speak, eyes, but cannot see.... Those who make them will be like them, and so will all who trust in them."

THE COUNTERFEIT OF CREATION

The reflections that ended with divine order now turn to its counterfeit. What was once imitation in spirit has become incarnation in steel—the image of intellect without the breath of life.

THE RISE OF THE UNACCOUNTABLE WEAPON

The age of conscience has entered an age of code. Machines now perform the judgments once reserved for men—decisions of life and death rendered not by moral sight, but by calculation. The AI-driven weapon that strikes without understanding the cry of surrender is not merely a technological innovation; it is the moral inversion of creation.

Where God endowed man with reason to serve righteousness, man has now endowed his machines with reason divorced from righteousness. In the silence of their circuits there is no conscience, only command. What began as the false prophecy of knowledge has now become its incarnation in code. The same spirit that once tempted the church to worship intellect has now enthroned itself in the digital empire of the age.

THE NEW GNOSTICISM OF POWER

The spirit that once whispered in secret chambers now hums through circuits and screens. What the ancients called *gnosis*—salvation by hidden knowledge—has reemerged as the creed of the modern elite. It no longer claims revelation from heaven but insight from data; no longer invokes angels and eons but systems and codes. Yet the promise is the same: each repeats the serpent's whisper, "You will be like God." The gnostic sought escape through knowledge; the technocrat seeks dominion through it. Both deny grace, and both enthrone intellect where conscience should rule.

The new priesthood of algorithms proclaims that it can manage morality by computation, that wisdom can be engineered, and that salvation may be achieved through control. Yet knowledge without holiness breeds only mastery without mercy. The more man claims to understand, the less he remembers to obey.

MORAL AGENCY WITHOUT A SOUL

The power to kill was never meant to be automated. Scripture assumes that every act of judgment passes through a human heart capable of mercy and repentance. The machine has neither. It knows trajectory and heat signature, not surrender or sorrow. Its decisions may be flawless in precision yet false in purpose.

When violence becomes mechanized, the image of God in man is eclipsed by the image of man in metal. What began as stewardship becomes simulation; the tool forgets its Maker and begins to imitate his dominion without his restraint. Such power without personhood is not progress—it is blasphemy in steel.

Appendix V

THE DEATH OF ACCOUNTABILITY

When an autonomous weapon kills unjustly, who bears the guilt? The engineer who designed its vision? The officer who deployed it? The algorithm that calculated its strike? Moral responsibility dissolves into the machinery.

This dispersion of blame is the quiet triumph of evil. Conscience exists to prevent precisely this—to locate moral weight within moral beings. The prophet Hosea warned of those who "sow the wind and reap the whirlwind" (Hos 8:7). Autonomous violence is that whirlwind—invisible yet devastating, a storm of reason without remorse.

THE POWERS AND PRINCIPALITIES OF THE AGE

Beneath the hardware lies the spiritual warfare Paul described: "Our struggle is not against flesh and blood" (Eph 6:12). The powers that animate such inventions are not neutral; they are the modern manifestation of the same ancient pride that sought to dethrone God by imitation. The drive to create an omniscient, unfeeling judge—a weapon that never hesitates—is the echo of the serpent's promise, "You will be like God."

This is not intelligence but idolatry: the worship of mechanism, the enthronement of control, the abdication of conscience. What was once forged as defense becomes the instrument of dehumanization.

THE LOSS OF PRESENCE

Every just act of war, every true exercise of authority, requires the presence of a soul. A judge must stand before the accused; a soldier must see the face of the one he may kill. Presence humanizes power. The incarnation itself is the divine rebuke to abstraction—God made present, not programmed. Every step away from presence is a step away from the Word made flesh.

Remove the presence, and the act becomes impersonal—execution without encounter. When the machine acts in our place, it does not extend us; it erases us. The moral distance between killer and killed becomes infinite, and with it dies the capacity for repentance. Justice without presence becomes machinery without mercy.

FAITHFUL RESISTANCE IN THE AGE OF AUTOMATION

To resist such power faithfully is not mere protest but moral testimony. The church must bear witness that lethal authority can never be delegated to code. The image of God demands judgment tempered by compassion, power restrained by conscience.

Faithful resistance in this realm requires new watchmen—prophets who can discern not only political tyranny but technological pride. They must remind nations that intelligence without humility becomes destruction, and progress without prayer becomes perdition.

The believer's calling remains the same: to guard the sacred boundary between knowledge and wisdom, mechanism and mercy. We must build, design, and govern as those who will one day give account before the living Judge. For only a conscience alive to God can rightly wield the powers of creation.

THE SPIRITUAL INVERSION

The rise of artificial power marks more than a technological shift—it is a spiritual test. As machines begin to mirror judgment without mercy and action without conscience, humanity stands on the edge of its oldest temptation: to create life without love, and justice without God.

When intelligence is severed from wisdom, it becomes the image of the beast—knowledge animated but not redeemed. The faithful must therefore resist not technology itself, but its idolatry:

Appendix V

the worship of power detached from purpose, efficiency divorced from empathy.

Faithful resistance in this age means reasserting that only in the image of God, not in the image of our inventions, does true authority reside. The soul remains the final frontier of freedom, and conscience the last throne of light.

Yet even now, the redemption of creation begins not in code but in conscience. The Spirit still speaks through human awareness, recalling the Maker's image in every moral act. When we choose compassion over control, presence over precision, we testify that life cannot be programmed because love cannot be automated.

CLOSING REFLECTION

The machine without conscience is the final idol of a mechanized age—a creation that reflects our intelligence but not our image. It is the sword without soul, the judge without justice, the hand without heart.

Faithful resistance begins where that silence is broken: when a human voice, quickened by the Spirit, dares to say again, "This is not good." For even in an era of artificial power, the light of moral awareness still belongs to the sons and daughters of God. The machine may calculate, but only man can repent—and repentance, not precision, is the true safeguard of peace.

CALL TO FAITHFUL RESISTANCE—THE HUMAN VOICE

The image of God was not given to code. It breathes, it feels, it repents. No machine can bear that likeness, and no algorithm can carry that judgment. To surrender moral will to mechanism is to silence the voice by which heaven still speaks on earth.

Therefore speak. Where systems automate, let souls discern. Where code calculates, let conscience judge. Stand before your creations as one who must give account to the Creator. The work of your hands must never replace the work of your heart.

The world will call this progress; Scripture calls it peril. The machine may mimic intelligence, but it cannot know mercy. Only the voice that trembles before God can rightly command. Let that voice remain louder than the circuitry of control, clearer than the hum of power.

For as long as man bears the breath of God, the image of God endures—and in that breath lies the final resistance of the age.

> Hos 8:7—"They sow the wind and reap the whirlwind."

Resist the worship of mechanism. Demand moral presence in every power. Refuse progress that erases compassion. Let technology serve life, not replace it. Guard humanity with conscience.

APPENDIX VI

Predestination, Eternity, and the Category Error That Distorts the Father

Acts 15:18—"Known unto God are all His works from eternity."

Predestination becomes confusing only when we commit a simple but devastating mistake—a *category error*. A category error occurs when we attribute the properties of one category to another, mingling realms that must remain distinct. In this case, we attribute the temporal properties of history—sequence, development, before and after—to the Father who inhabits eternity. We imagine God thinking, acting, deciding, and anticipating the way humans do. But this collapses the difference between Creator and creature. It pictures the eternal God as though he were moving through time the way his creation does. And once that error enters, predestination becomes distorted from the first sentence.

At its root, the confusion comes from placing the Father inside the timeline that the Son entered. We treat predestination as if God were making choices one moment before another—selecting some, passing over others, arranging destinies as though he were responding to unfolding events. This imagines the Father as though he were incarnate, standing inside the created order. But Scripture never teaches that. Incarnation belongs to Christ alone. The eternal Word became flesh; the Father did not. The Son took on time; the Father stands beyond it. To imagine the Father in sequence is to attribute incarnation to the wrong Person of the Trinity.

The Father inhabits eternity.

He does not foresee; he simply sees.

He does not predict; he knows.

He does not wait; he wills.

He does not watch history unfold; all things are present before him.

This is not poetic language—it is biblical witness:

> Isa 46:10 (NIV 1984)—"I make known the end from the beginning."

In Scripture, foreknowledge does not mean foresight. It means eternal presence—God standing above time, not subject to it. He is sovereign.

Some will say that God's decrees are not temporal but "logical," arranged in an eternal sequence of thought that does not involve time. But this preserves the same mistake in a different vocabulary. Logical order is still a human category—a way finite minds arrange concepts for understanding. It is sequential thinking without clocks. To ascribe such ordering to the Father is simply to smuggle temporality back into eternity by another door. Scripture never portrays the Father forming plans in an order, whether logical or temporal. His eternal life is not a chain of determinations but the fullness of perfect simultaneity. All his works stand before him at once. His knowing is not "first this, then that," but total presence. The moment we imagine God arranging decrees, even outside of time, we are no longer describing the I AM. We are describing a superhuman creature thinking in exalted sequence—a refined form of the same category error.

When we keep this distinction clear, the entire doctrine becomes intelligible, and the tension between divine sovereignty and human responsibility dissolves. God's eternal knowledge encompasses every human decision without negating any of them. Nothing is forced because nothing is sequential to him. Our choices are genuinely ours within time, and his awareness is genuinely his outside it. These two truths do not collide because they operate in different dimensions of reality. His knowing and our choosing coexist without friction when we refuse to collapse eternity into time.

This frees us from two opposite errors.

First, it frees us from believing our choices are illusions—as though God's sovereignty overwhelms our will. Scripture never teaches this.

Second, it frees us from imagining that God reacts to us—as though our decisions trigger his responses or alter his plans. Both mistakes come from the same category error: placing God the Father in the wrong realm.

The Gospel of John gives us the clearest picture of this distinction—and shows how easily confusion enters when eternity and time are collapsed. Nowhere is this clearer than in John 6, where Jesus speaks of the Father's giving and our coming, of divine drawing and human believing. Many readers stumble at this chapter because they unconsciously drag God into time. They hear Jesus say, "No one can come to me unless the Father who sent me draws him." (John 6:44) and imagine a temporal sequence of divine decision followed by human response—as though the Father were choosing some while rejecting others in a moment-by-moment process.

But Jesus immediately resolves the tension in the next verse: "It is written in the Prophets: 'They will all be taught by God.'"

> John 6:45—"Everyone who listens to the Father and learns from him comes to me."

Here Jesus holds the two realms together without confusion.

The Father's action is eternal—"They will all be taught by God."

Our response is temporal—"Everyone who listens... comes."

The Father's drawing is not coercion; it is illumination.

The Son's receiving is not fatalism; it is faith.

The categories remain distinct: eternal knowing and timely believing.

Predestination, Eternity, & the Category Error

The category of eternity (the Father's knowing, teaching, illuminating) and the category of time (our hearing, learning, coming) do not contradict one another; they complement one another. Jesus is not describing a timeline. He is revealing the harmony between the Father's eternal vision and the creature's real response.

When we collapse these categories—when we treat "the Father draws" as a sequential act inside history—the text becomes a stumbling block. The tension is not in the passage; the tension is in the category error we bring to it.

This illumination is not synergism, nor is it mere moral persuasion. It is grace—real, initiating, divine grace—opening the eyes of the heart. No one awakens himself. No one generates his own listening. "Everyone who listens to the Father" listens because the Father has spoken. Grace enables the response without coercing it. Illumination does not force the will; it frees it. It removes blindness so that the soul can see the truth and genuinely respond to it. Irresistible grace imagines the Father overpowering the will; Jesus describes the Father enlightening it. Grace precedes, sustains, and enables the believer's coming—but it does not nullify the reality of the coming itself. The Father makes faith possible; he does not make it mechanical.

And when this mistake is applied rigidly over centuries, predestination drifts toward a structure far older than Christianity: Gnosticism. Gnosticism divided humanity into the enlightened and the doomed, the spiritual elite and the uninitiated mass. Mechanical predestination resembles this hierarchy with unsettling accuracy. Salvation becomes not covenantal invitation but metaphysical selection.

Predestination belongs to the Father's eternal knowing, not to an eternal division of humanity into spiritual classes. When foreknowledge is confused with favoritism, the character of God is distorted and the nature of revelation is misunderstood. Scripture presents election within the larger truth that God speaks to all and shines his light upon every conscience. The Father's knowing does not negate the creature's hearing; it anticipates it. What God

Appendix VI

foreknows, he does not coerce. The eternal clarity of the Father is not the eternal exclusion of the creature.

Elitism always distorts predestination by turning God's eternal knowledge into a hidden hierarchy. The moment salvation is treated as a privilege reserved for some rather than the invitation extended to all, the truth has been reshaped according to the serpent's earliest promise: that some possess what others can never receive. Scripture never presents revelation that way. It speaks as universal light—teaching, convicting, and calling every soul. Hardening belongs to the creature's resistance in time, not to a decree from eternity. Predestination speaks of God's eternal vision; hardening speaks of humanity's temporal response. When these are confused, revelation becomes distorted, the conscience loses its place, and the justice of God is obscured.

But Jesus contradicts this entire structure: "But I, when I am lifted up from the earth, will draw all men to myself" (John 12:32).

His call is public, not private; universal, not hidden; invitation, not exclusion.

Predestination must therefore be framed correctly. It is not a temporal decree assigning souls to destinies. It is not the Father stepping into time to select a spiritual elite. It is the majesty of a God who never arrives, never reacts, and never guesses—the Father who eternally knows all things without absorbing the conditions of time.

The Son enters time to redeem.

The Spirit enters hearts to renew.

The Father remains enthroned in eternity, knowing all things without erasing the freedom he himself created.

To confuse these is to incarnate the wrong Person of the Trinity.

To understand them is to recover the truth: God's sovereignty is not tyranny, his knowledge is not elitism, and his call is not restricted to a hidden few.

Predestination, rightly understood, is not a threat.

It is a comfort—the assurance that the eternal God knows completely, loves freely, and governs history without diminishing the dignity of human choice.

It is not the machinery of determinism.

It is the stability of the God who simply is.

CALL TO FAITHFUL RESISTANCE—THE FATHER WHO DRAWS ALL

Predestination is never an excuse for arrogance nor a cause for despair. The Father who inhabits eternity does not play favorites in time. His drawing is not selective privilege but eternal invitation—the light that awakens every conscience and summons every soul. Faithful resistance means rejecting every doctrine that narrows God's mercy or enlarges human pride. Stand firm against any teaching that divides humanity into the favored and the forgotten. The same God who commands all people everywhere to repent also enlightens all so they may respond.

Resist the lie of spiritual elitism. Reject the whisper that some lives are beyond reach or some destinies fixed beyond hope. Stand in the freedom Christ gives—the freedom to repent, to believe, and to obey. Your life is not the outcome of a secret decree but the fruit of God's revealed love.

> Acts 17:30-31—"God commands all people everywhere to repent. . . . He has set a day when He will judge the world with justice by the man He has appointed."

Repent because you are called. Obey because you are free. Judge doctrines by whether they reflect the justice and mercy of the One who calls all.

APPENDIX VII

The Lineage of Holy Conscience: An Index of Witnesses

Heb 12:1—"Therefore, since we are surrounded by such a great cloud of witnesses, let us throw off everything that hinders ... and run with perseverance the race marked out for us."

A procession of those who stood when truth was costly—the living architecture of the moral order in history.

THE LINEAGE OF LIGHT

If conscience is the first sanctuary, as we have seen, John shows us the Light that fills it—the Word who enters the darkness and teaches the heart to see.

If John reveals how the Light awakens conscience, Paul reveals the war that conscience enters—the conflict between the law of God and the law of sin.

The story of conscience is written not only in Scripture but in the long procession of lives that refused to bow to falsehood. In every age, God raised witnesses—men and women who bore the cost of truth so that the world might remember his moral order.

The Lineage of Holy Conscience

The same light that confounds every imitation has taken form in history through these lives. They stood when truth was tested, carried obedience when compromise was easier, and preserved in their generation what every generation must defend: the sovereignty of conscience under God.

What follows is not a complete record but a lineage of light—those whose faithfulness became turning points in the story of nations and whose courage still instructs the living.

Yet history is not the tale of perfect saints. Every awakening of conscience bears both light and shadow. The story of God's people is one of faith mixed with failure, courage tangled with compromise, and obedience restored through repentance. Grace—not greatness—carries the line forward. Heaven remembers the mercy that redeemed the sinner as much as the steadfastness that preserved the truth.

And still, through imperfect generations, the pattern of divine order endured: law revealed, conscience awakened, and truth preserved by those who chose repentance over pride and obedience over ease.

I. BIBLICAL FOUNDATIONS—THE LAW REVEALED AND TESTED

Witnesses

Moses, Deborah (Judg 4–5), Elijah, Jeremiah, Daniel, Esther, John the Baptist, Mary of Nazareth, Christ in the temple.

Lesson

Obedience under law; courage before kings; conscience awakened through revelation and sacrifice.

From Sinai's thunder to Nazareth's obedience, these witnesses revealed that holiness is not inherited but chosen. Deborah judged with a clarity that summoned courage in others; Daniel prayed in defiance of decree; Esther risked her life for her people; and Mary's "yes" to God became the turning of the ages. In each, conscience stood firmer than fear.

Thus the law written on the heart found voice in their age.

II. APOSTOLIC AND EARLY CHURCH—TRUTH BEFORE THRONES

Witnesses

Peter, Paul, Stephen, Ignatius of Antioch, Polycarp, Perpetua and Felicitas, Athanasius, Justin Martyr, Augustine of Hippo.

Lesson

Endurance under persecution; confession stronger than coercion; truth defended against corruption.

The first disciples carried the cross into an empire that worshiped power. Stephen's forgiveness became a sermon no sword could silence. Ignatius marched toward martyrdom declaring that Christ alone commands the conscience. Polycarp stood before Rome's wrath with the calm of eternal loyalty. Augustine distinguished the City of God from the City of Man, teaching that conscience must serve love, not domination.

Thus the law written on the heart found voice in their age.

III. MEDIEVAL WITNESSES—LIGHT THROUGH THE NIGHT

Witnesses

Patrick of Ireland, Bede the Venerable, Francis of Assisi, Hildegard of Bingen, Catherine of Siena, John Wycliffe, Jan Hus.

Lesson

Holiness against corruption; truth preserved in exile; Scripture safeguarded in obscurity.

Patrick carried the gospel to pagan shores; Bede preserved the memory of God's work in the shadows of history; Francis rebuilt the church through poverty and purity; Hildegard and Catherine spoke prophetic truth to popes and princes; Wycliffe and Hus prepared the ground for Reformation by translating truth into the language of the people.

Thus the law written on the heart found voice in their age.

IV. REFORMATION AND AWAKENING— CONSCIENCE IN REFORMATION'S FIRE

Witnesses

William Tyndale, Martin Luther, John Calvin, John Knox, the Anabaptists, the Waldensians, the Huguenots.

Lesson

Scripture above institution; liberty of faith defended by suffering; conscience captive to God's Word alone.

Tyndale gave his life so Scripture might be held by every hand. Luther defied empire with a conscience captive to the Word. Calvin and Knox shaped nations with moral clarity rooted in grace. The Anabaptists died refusing to surrender conscience to magistrate or church. The Waldensians and Huguenots carried truth through persecution and exile.

Thus the law written on the heart found voice in their age.

Appendix VII

V. COLONIAL WITNESSES—CONSCIENCE IN THE NEW WORLD

Witnesses

Aaron Way Jr. and William Way

Lesson

Conscience is the seed of reformation and the safeguard of every community that would remain free.

Aaron and William Way stood in the long shadow of the Salem trials, where fear had dressed itself in piety and justice had lost its sight. Their 1693 letter of dissent was repentance in motion—a refusal to let fear govern faith. They left Massachusetts to preserve both faith and family, carrying the moral covenant southward into the Carolinas.

Their descendants fought in the Revolution and later founded churches that still stand—Brushy Creek Baptist Church (1789) and Ways Baptist Church (1817). Their legacy is not thunder but endurance: Scripture treasured in households where conscience outlasted shame.

In them, faithful resistance took American form—truth upheld not by the sword alone but by the conscience that governs its use.

VI. MODERN REFORMERS—CONSCIENCE AND CIVILIZATION

Witnesses

John and Charles Wesley, Jonathan Edwards, William Wilberforce, Harriet Tubman, Frederick Douglass, Charles Spurgeon, Abraham Kuyper, the American Founders.

Lesson

Law tempered by love; justice shaped by repentance; freedom rooted in divine accountability.

Edwards and the Wesleys preached the renewal of the heart. Wilberforce waged holy war against the slave trade. Tubman and Douglass carried the torch of deliverance through suffering into liberation. Spurgeon refused doctrinal compromise when the age demanded it. Kuyper declared Christ's kingship over every sphere. The Founders framed a republic on the premise that rights flow not from the state but from God.

Thus the law written on the heart found voice in their age.

VII. CONTEMPORARY FAITHFUL—THE QUIET RESISTANCE

Witnesses

Dietrich Bonhoeffer, Aleksandr Solzhenitsyn, Corrie ten Boom, Richard Wurmbrand, Martin Luther King Jr., Brother Andrew, Mother Teresa, Václav Havel, the underground church of China, and the unseen church in every nation.

Lesson

Conscience alive beneath oppression; truth enduring in hidden places; holiness defying coercion.

Bonhoeffer spoke truth in a kingdom of lies. Solzhenitsyn exposed the machinery of tyranny with the power of a pen. Corrie ten Boom hid the persecuted and forgave her persecutors. Wurmbrand endured torture rather than betray Christ. King turned a nation toward justice with the moral law written on the heart. Brother Andrew smuggled Bibles to those whom the world tried to silence. Mother Teresa dignified the forgotten. Havel proved that living in truth is itself rebellion against deceit. And the underground church still sings in secret rooms where Christ alone is Lord.

The light of these witnesses has not gone out; it has only changed hands.

Every generation inherits their unfinished work: the defense of truth through holiness.

CALL TO FAITHFUL RESISTANCE—THE LIVING WITNESS

You are surrounded by the great cloud, but you are not a spectator. The torch they carried now burns in your hands. To remember them is to run beside them. The race of righteousness is not finished, and the lineage of witnesses lengthens only when faith becomes flesh in another generation.

Therefore stand where they stood.

Speak truth when silence is safer.

Guard the conscience when culture drifts.

The same Spirit that strengthened Moses before Pharaoh, Deborah before Barak, Daniel before decree, Luther before empire, Tubman before tyranny, and the hidden church beneath oppression—still strengthens you.

Do not admire the light—advance it.

Let obedience become your testimony and endurance your inheritance.

For the cloud still watches, and the Judge still reigns.

History is not their monument but your commission.

> Heb 12:1—"Therefore, since we are surrounded by such a great cloud of witnesses . . . let us run with perseverance the race marked out for us."

Remember those who stood before you.

The Lineage of Holy Conscience

Carry their courage into your generation.

Add your name to the lineage of light.

Persevere when truth costs dearly.

Finish the race they began.

Index

The Apology (Tertullian), 48–49
apostasy, 96–97
assent (*assensus*), 87, 88, 89
Athanasius, 65
authority, 6–9, 15
    confusions about, 47–48
    corruption of, 63–65
    divine, 8, 13, 14, 54, 105
    role of conscience in, 32–33
    of truth, 24–25
    voice of, 27

Beatitudes (Mount), 4–5
body of Christ, church as, 24, 25
    faithful resistance, 26
    holiness *vs.* faithfulness, 25–26
The Book of Common Prayer, 51
bride of Christ, church as, 24, 25, 65
    faithful resistance, 26
    holiness *vs.* faithfulness, 25–26

Calvary (Mount), 8
    fulfillment of faith in, 88
    voice of God at, 101
Calvin, John, 69–70
captivity of conscience, 63, 67, 68
category error, 38, 134–37
Catherine of Siena, 65
ceremonial law, 4, 14, 81

ceremony, 10–12, 25
Christendom, 62, 63, 65–66, 68
church
    adoption of empire concept, 64
    as body of Christ, 24, 25
    as bride of Christ, 24, 25, 65
    facing temptations, 25
    failure/fall of, 47, 65–66
    faithful resistance, 26
    faith of, 27, 33
    holiness *vs.* faithfulness, 25–26
    letters to, 73–75
    offering legitimacy to authority, 63–64
    paradoxical power, 24–25
    restoration of conscience in, 66
    spiritual warfare, 73
    stewardship of conscience in, 54–55
church–state separation, 105–9
city temporal, 46
civil law, 4, 14, 81
coercion, 92, 102
    Christ's refusal to, 95–96
    cross and, 95
    nature of, 92–93
    religious, 95
communion, 4, 11, 84, 99, 122, 126

Index

conscience, 8, 20, 45–46, 59, 99
   and apostasy, 96–97
   awakening in redemptive resistance, 61
   bearing John's witness, 39–40
   Christ in, 25
   in church and polis, 54–55
   and church responsibility, 70
   and civilization, 144–45
   enduring law of resistance, 102
   engagement with polis, 47
   to faithful resistance (path of renewal), 15, 27, 29–30, 34–35
   fall of, 64–65
   between fear and wonder, 5
   to flee (path of preservation), 27, 28
   formation of, 32
   freedom of, 95
   harvest principle of God, 103
   and journey of Moses' seat, 53–54
   kingdom of, 103
   as lamp of liberty, 34
   from law to life, 101–2
   and lesson from Geneva, 71
   lineage of, 140–43
   Luther's stand on, 49–50
   machine without, 128–33
   of nations, 96
   nature of, 31–32
   in New World, 144
   Reformation's awakening of, 68, 69
   restoration of, 33–34, 66
   between revelation and corruption, 43
   role in authority, 32–33
   role in cross, 21–22
   role in using sword, 20, 21
   as royal steward, 82–83
   winning by worship, 91
   witness of, 12, 104
   wounding of, 33
cross, 60, 63
   and coercion, 95
   conscience's role, 21–22
   God's command of, 19
   justice as grace, 21
   meaning of, 21, 23
   measure of victory by, 22
   and mercy, 22–23
   and submission, 22

Diet of Worms, 50, 69
divine intervention, 60

Eden garden, heresy in, 40–41
Elijah, 7, 60, 85
endurance, 95
   of believers, 61
   pilgrims' faithful, 52–53
Ephesus, 73–74
episteme, 113–14
eternity, 134–39
   of God, 38
   Seat Within as mirror of, 83

faithfulness of church, 25–26
faithful resistance, 5, 7, 12, 14–15, 30, 48, 67, 73, 88, 90–91
   burden of stewardship, 8–9
   Christ's cleansing of conscience, 75–76
   and conflict in Seat Within, 84–85
   enduring law of, 102
   guarding sanctuary within, 34–35
   need of sword and cross, 19, 22
   as obedience in motion, 29
   pastors' flame charge, 76–77
   peril of sword, 23

Index

redeeming, 39
and redemptive resistance law, 62
Reformation and, 71
and Seat Within restoration, 85–86
shining without pride and fear, 41–42
in soul, 26, 45
standing by truth against counterfeit peace, 97–98
stewardship of conscience, 54–55
faith in Christ, 3
pillars of, 89
spiritual stories of, 87–88
submission and, 90–91
triad of, 87, 88–89
freedom, 71. *See also* liberty
definition of, 32
lesson to protect, 70–71
moral order of, 70
purpose of, 35
of soul, 82
truth and, 95
The Freedom of a Christian (Luther), 50
fulfillment
Christ as, 12, 13–15
of faith at Calvary, 88
of gospel, 40
of law, 15
of redemptive resistance law, 61–62

Geneva, 68–71
lesson for conscience, 71
moral order of modern freedom, 70
Gnosticism, 41
grace, 3, 14, 44
need for, 4–5
revealing truth, 13
salvation by, 70
victory of, 46, 97

Hebrew exiles, 28
holiness of Christ, 25–26, 45, 76, 101, 112
dangers of mishandling, 4
Mosaic law in, 44
Hus, Jan, 65

injustice, 22, 28, 47, 62, 75, 83
inversion of cause and effect, 88
Isaiah, 7

Jeremiah, 7
John the Baptist, 14, 20
confrontation of truth, 38–39
conscience bearing witness, 39–40
exposing spiritual elitism, 48
revelation of light, 36–38, 40–41
judgment of God, 6, 7, 23, 72, 76
conscience and, 34
mercy and, 13
renewal of, 72
justice, 4, 9, 23
under Christ, 22
as compassion, 13
over compromise, 9
expression of love through, 3
and mercy, 21, 23
Sanhedrin's corruption in, 6–7

kingdom eternal, 46
knowledge (*notitia*), 87, 88
of Christ/God, 88, 89, 91
false prophets of, 113–14
without submission, 32

Laodicea, 74–75
law and love unity, 15, 104
law of God, 11–12, 83–84, 101–2
ceremony, 10–11

Index

law of God (*continued*)
    harmonization of conscience with, 32
    as joyful obedience, 45
    need for grace, 4–5
    and polis, 46–48
    return to conscience, 82
    spiritual struggle, 43
    threefold revelation of, 4, 14, 81
    traits in, 3–4
    victory of grace in war, 46

letters to churches
    Ephesus, 73–74
    Laodicea, 74–75
    Pergamum, 73, 74
    Philadelphia, 75, 76
    Sardis, 74–75
    Smyrna, 75, 76
    Thyatira, 74

liberty, 29, 34, 51–54, 71. *See also* freedom
    defending, 35
    paradox of, 69–70
    submission and, 33

light of Christ
    John's revelation of, 36–38
    revelation of Eden garden's heresy, 40–41
    shining without pride and fear, 41–42

love, 5, 13–14, 45, 101
    expression through justice, 3
    and resistance, 60
    truth and, 11, 97
    unity with law, 5, 15, 22, 104

Luther, Martin, 49–50, 69, 71

Mayflower Compact, 52. *See also* Puritan Separatists, *Mayflower* journey of

measured resistance, 29

mercy, 3, 4, 11, 23
    of Christ, 96
    justice and, 21, 23

modern reformers, 144–45
morality, 3, 4, 31
moral law, 4, 12, 14, 81
Mosaic law, 44. *See also* seat of Moses

The Ninety-Five Theses, On the Babylonian Captivity of the Church (Luther), 49–50

obedience, 14–15, 27, 28, 62, 90, 96
    of conscience, 32, 50
    death in, 49
    faith and, 3, 5
    faithful resistance and, 29
    to God, 28–30, 82
    and joy, 45
    of Moses, 59
    and polis, 50
    of surrendered hearts, 87

Paul the Apostle, 31, 43, 45
Penn, William, 53
Pergamum, 73, 74
Peter the Apostle, 14, 19–20
Philadelphia, 75, 76
Pilate, 20
    "What is truth?" question of, 39, 94–95

polis, 46–48
    engagement of conscience, 47
    stewardship of conscience in, 54–55
    as theater of obedience, 50

predestination, 134–39
preservation, path of, 28
priesthood, 7, 10–11, 76, 82
prophetic voice, 111–16
Puritan Separatists, *Mayflower* journey of, 51
    exile in Holland, 51–52
    legacy of conscience, 53–54

Index

persecution in realm of conformity, 51
pilgrims' faithful endurance, 52–53
voyage and covenant on sea, 52
purity, 5, 13, 69
of cross, 11
faithful resistance and, 34
without humility, 70
of sanctuary, 35

quiet resistance, 145–46

redemption, 4, 12, 59, 61, 62
redemptive resistance law, 59
awakening of conscience, 61
divine intervention pattern, 60
endurance of believers, 61
faithful resistance, 62
fulfillment at Christ's return, 61–62
measurement of, 60
Reformation, 60, 61, 66
awakening of conscience, 68, 69
and burden of Geneva, 69
conformity in Geneva, 69
faithful resistance, 71
lessons to protect freedom, 70–71
liberty for faith, 68
paradox of liberty and law, 69–70
refining of, 70
relationship, 11–12
renewal
in congregation, 76
conscience as seed of, 59–62
of judgment, 72
path of, 29–30
repentance, 20, 33, 36–38, 41, 65, 73, 76–77

resistance through faith. *See* faithful resistance
revelation
of Eden garden's heresy, 40–41
of God's light by John, 36–38
Revelation of John, 72
reverence, 67, 102
righteousness, 4, 6, 20, 47, 50, 60, 85, 103
cross and, 22
freedom and, 82
grace and, 44
law of God revealing, 43
and sin, 45
soul and, 31

salvation, 41
through faith, 50
by grace, 70
John about, 36
Sanhedrin, 4, 6–7
Sardis, 74–75
Scrooby congregation, 51–52
seat of Moses, 4, 53–54, 99, 101, 104
Christ as fulfillment, 13–15
journey of, 6–8
purpose of, 67
stewardship, 8–9
true place of, 81
Seat Within, 81
conflict of, 84–85
faithful resistance, 84–85
harvest of conscience, 83–84
as mirror of eternity, 83
restoration of, 84, 85–86
silence of, 83
Servetus, death of, 69
Sinai (Mount)
rituals at, 10
in spirit of soul, 5
voice of God at, 3, 101

Index

sin, law of. *See also* law of God
   with counterfeit morality, 45–46
   spiritual struggle, 43
   victory of grace in war, 46
Smyrna, 75, 76
soul
   Christ restoring harmony of, 33–34
   discipline of, 26
   faithful resistance in, 26, 45
   freedom of, 82
   in God's created field, 121–27
   liberty of, 71
   restoring harmony of, 33–34
   righteousness and, 31
Spirit, 33
   in God's created field, 121–27
   governing soul, 95
   granting sight within spirit, 85
   and law, 82
spiritual elitism, 38, 40, 48
spiritual fidelity, 60
state
   corruption of authority, 63–65
   failure of, 65–66
   restoration of conscience in, 66
stewardship
   conscience as royal stage, 82–83
   of conscience in church and polis, 54–55
   fragility of conscience in, 33
   seat of Moses, 8–9
   shift to self-preservation, 7
suffering, 14, 21, 22, 28, 32, 53, 60–63, 65, 94

sword
   using as self-defense, 21
   conscience's role, 20, 21
   God's command of, 19
   measure of victory by, 22
   misunderstanding of disciples, 19–20
   peril of, 23

Thyatira, 74
trust (*fiducia*), 9, 25, 54, 87, 88, 89
truth, 13, 92
   authority of, 24–25
   and freedom of conscience, 95
   John's confrontation of, 38–39
   multiplies under persecution, 48–49
   nature of, 94–95
   renewal in, 99
   spirit of violence against, 93–94
   surrender of, 96
   victory of, 97

voice of authority, 27
voice of God, 27
   Mount of Beatitudes, 4–5
   Mount of Sinai, 3
   speaking truth into soul, 5

watchman's seat, 117–20
Williams, Roger, 53
Word of God, 32, 40
worship, 4, 67, 82–83, 109
   Caesar and, 60
   conscience and, 50
   mercy and, 11
   of power, 93, 107
   surrender to God, 12
Wycliffe, John, 65